# WINDOWS ON SOCIAL SPIRITUALITY

Jesuit Centre for Faith and Justice

# Windows on Social Spirituality

the columba press

First published in 2003 by
the columba press
55A Spruce Avenue, Stillorgan Industrial Park,
Blackrock, Co Dublin


Cover by Bill Bolger
Origination by The Columba Press
Printed in Ireland by ColourBooks Ltd, Dublin

ISBN 1 85607 400 5

# Contents

# Foreword

Most of us, most of the time, are at least a little aware that there is something wrong with our world that needs fixing. But it is a far cry from that awareness to sustained, passionate reflection and action to set things right. Why get started since it seems like such a huge task? Why persevere since there are so many disappointments along what seems like an endless journey? And really, is this the truth, that there is no end to this quest for a more just world?

These are the sorts of questions tackled in this book. The answers range from citing inspirational figures like Sonia O'Sullivan to a consideration of our 'off-centre' Trinitarian God, through consideration of the Spiritual Exercises of Saint Ignatius of Loyola, reflection on personal experiences of work for justice, considerations of theological themes like Church, Eucharist, Reconciliation, Mary and a philosophical critique of inadequate approaches to spirituality. The authors are all practitioners in the field and their experience and commitment are transparent in what they write. Equally transparent is their Christian faith – they write persuasively of how a Christian understanding of the world can motivate, nourish and sustain our efforts to bring about a more just world.

There are many possible motives for working for a better world – guilt, duty, fear, anger at injustice and so on. All of these have their validity. It is so refreshing, however, to read, time and again in this book, that beneath all these motives is the simple reality that we are loved by God and out of gratitude for this love we feel called to make our world more just. This is the principle and foundation of which Saint Ignatius speaks. The more we can live out of this atmosphere of love and gratitude the more likely it is that our struggle for justice will persevere for the 'long haul', and that we will be able to embark and continue on that 'long march' through the institutions and structures that a more just world order requires. Anger and duty on their own may easily lead to burn-out: when subsumed by love and trust in our faithful God they sustain life-long engagement.

Faith and justice are always embedded in a certain culture, an underlying and often unconscious system of values, meanings, assumptions and worldviews. In this book this culture is revealed as a spirituality, the different parts of which sparkle and attract like jewels on a necklace. It is with great pleasure that I commend the authors and the Jesuit Centre for Faith and Justice for producing this work and I warmly recommend it to readers.

*Gerry O'Hanlon, SJ*
*Provincial*

# CHAPTER ONE

# The Two Gardeners

## *Bill Toner SJ*

Imagine that you had to employ a gardener. You ask around among your friends and neighbours, and eventually you hear of two gardeners who are available. From people who have employed them, you are able to draw up the following profiles of the two.

The first gardener plants a variety of vegetables and flowers. Periodically he comes along and inspects them. Whenever he sees a plant or a flower that is not doing well he pulls it up and throws it on the compost heap or into the bin. He has planted plenty of seeds and plants, so this practice does not greatly affect the yield or the appearance of the garden. Small stunted and yellow cabbage plants, wallflowers that slugs have had a feed on, frost-bitten blossoms, all of these go out. There are a lot of advantages in this approach. The appearance of the garden is always pretty and healthy. And diseased plants do not get a chance to infect other plants.

The second gardener also plants a variety of vegetables and flowers and periodically inspects them. But his approach is different. He is on the lookout for plants that are not doing well to see what he can do to make them more healthy. If a cabbage is looking yellow, he gives it more feed. If a flower is attacked by slugs he puts down extra slug-killer. If some of the blossoms are frost-bitten he puts a glass cloche over them to protect them and give them a chance to recover. He hates to see any plant or flower dying. His gardens are not as nice-looking as those looked after by the first gardener, as some of the plants are clearly ailing.

If you wanted to employ a gardener you would almost certainly choose the first. The first strikes us as an efficient, practical, no-nonsense gardener. The second gardener seems soft-hearted, and is plant-centred rather than garden-centred. Except in the case of very rare plants, few of us would want to pay good money so that sickly specimens would be nursed, and perhaps the overall condition of the garden neglected.

## Images of God

When it comes to choosing between different images of God we find alternatives that are somewhat like the types of gardener proposed above. However, we may find to our surprise that the image of God that seems more in line with Christian faith is more like the second, inefficient, gardener than the first one. We can, as a kind of shorthand, describe the first as the God of 'reason' and the second as the God of 'revelation'. Of course, since revelation comes to us only with the help of human reason, it would be a mistake to draw a hard and fast line between the two images. But nevertheless we can draw a distinction between the images of God that are solely or mainly based on abstract and scientific reasoning, and ones that have as their basis the holy books. Believers see these books as 'inspired', meaning that God speaks to us through them. In the case of these holy books, the imagination and emotion of the authors, as well as their reason, plays a part.

The God of reason has been around at least since the time of the great Greek philosophers, such as Plato and Plotinus. In fact the First Vatican Council, building on centuries of Christian philosophy, taught that God can in principle be known by the natural light of human reason. Christian philosophers worked out 'proofs' for the existence of God.

The attempt to create a 'rational' image of God has particularly come into its own with the rise of modern science.

The Enlightenment saw the rise of 'Deism', which was proposed as a 'rational' alternative to traditional Christian faith in God. As more and more of the mysteries of the universe were found to have rational explanations, many scientists and philosophers of science began to question where God fitted into the picture, or even whether there was room for God at all. Modern cosmologists such as Stephen Hawking and Richard Dawkins have pondered the question of God in the context of a universe apparently originating in a Big Bang and then designed blindly by evolutionary forces. In fact, all modern cosmology really has a place for is a 'god of the gaps'. In other words where science comes to a point where no explanation can be found (such as who lit the fuse for the Big Bang) 'god' may be trotted out to fill the gap.

Because science is so dominant in modern life, our conception of God has become more and more shaped by the questions and debates of the scientists. If this debate does not actually lead us into agnosticism or atheism, we are at least in danger of constructing a God which is science-friendly, but without personality. This is very different from the images of God constructed by the writers of the psalms or the medieval mystics, who looked for God within themselves, or found him in the 'awe' of the universe.

The physical sciences are not the only discipline which shapes our view of how the world works. Increasingly modern economics has come to make us look at human behaviour in an increasingly rationalistic way. Economics has become a world with laws of its own independent of other norms of behaviour. 'Economic Man' is seen as an individual who follows only the dictates of his interest in personal gain. The notion of social justice is eliminated. Justice becomes 'commutative' justice which is bound only by the conventions of negotiated contracts within the framework of the law of supply and demand.

The modern God of reason may be a subject for academic

debate. But this God does not engage us in any personal way, or command our loyalty or affection. The whole thrust of modern scientific enquiry is to make God as impersonal as possible, rather like a giant computer, predictable, inflexible, and somehow even pre-programmed. God in this view is also rather like the first gardener described above, in that he (or 'it') is efficient in running the universe, but we do not expect him to be bothered with the minor details of human misdeeds and misfortunes.

## The Influence of Trent

Another factor that has deeply influenced our image of God has been the teaching of the Council of Trent in the areas of sin and confession. Trent reinforced the notion of a heavenly calculus, by which the gravity of sins was measured precisely, and punishment administered automatically. In the 1950s most Catholic schoolchildren would, by way of illustration of divine justice, have been presented with the paradox of the man who lived a blameless life, but late in life committed a sexual sin. The next day he was killed in a car crash. There was no doubt about his eternal fate. He would have gone straight to hell, as sexual sins were always 'mortal' sins, with no exceptions. In this presentation of sin there was no discussion of what view God might take of the man's misfortune. Indeed the impression was given that God was powerless in the situation, bound by rules which may have been ultimately his, but which had now been tidied up and fastened down by his earthly delegates. God was depicted in the same way as a human judge who, in the case of particular crimes, has no option but to pronounce the death penalty or other determinate penalty.

In the heyday of 'fixed penalty' offences, there were some priests who held out some hope of a more flexible approach by God. During retreats little anecdotes were told about God's mercy and the power of grace. But in general, it was suggested that the only hope lay in some type of 'death-bed' repentance, where the sinner managed to summon up the contrition necessary to strike out the offence. Again, it was not really up to God. The responsibility was the sinner's.

There can be little doubt that his kind of theology deeply influenced the popular image of God. At worst God was reduced to the level of a robot, applying sanctions with the cold impersonality and rationality of a traffic warden writing a parking ticket. It reinforced the 'scientific' notion of a God without personality and with only a passive role in a universe governed by moral as well as scientific laws.

## The God of Christian Revelation

The God of revelation is very different from the God of reason. In the holy books, God is far from impersonal. We find all kinds of emotions and attitudes attributed to God in the Bible. Some of these are not very attractive, such as jealousy, impetuousness, vindictiveness, favouritism, unpredictability and so on. But the outstanding qualities that come through, taking the Bible in its entirety, are love and mercy.

The God of revelation is in fact rather similar to the second gardener described above. Indeed the Bible frequently uses images of plants and plant-care to illustrate the solicitude of God: 'A bruised reed he will not break' (Isaiah 42:3). The Bible is full of images of a God who seems to be more interested in the individual than in the overall system. The New Testament constantly employs the metaphor of the lost sheep: 'Suppose a man has a hundred sheep and one of them strays; will he not leave the ninety-nine on the hillside and go in search of the stray?' (Mt 18:12). Just as the second gardener was plant-centred rather than garden-centred, so the God of revelation is depicted as having a special concern for the weak, the poor, the lost, the blind, the sick, rather than for the overall efficiency of 'the system'.

This is not an image of God that could be worked out by scientific reasoning or logic. The God of revelation is, frankly, a very peculiar God. Terms like 'soft-hearted' and 'woolly-headed' come to mind. Even practising Christians can react negatively to some of the more extreme examples of Christ's concern for the 'losers' such as the son who ran off and wasted his money, or the workers in the vineyard who strolled in just before closing time. Nobody recognised the 'scandal' of the God revealed in Jesus better than St Paul, imbued as he was with the 'logic' of Greek philosophy: 'While the Jews demand miracles, and the Greeks look for wisdom [a term used by Paul for the human wisdom of philosophy and rhetoric], here are we preaching a crucified Christ; to the Jews an obstacle that they cannot get over, to the pagans madness' (1 Cor 1:22-3).

## The God who is 'Off-Centre'

If we look at the world and the universe through the eyes of science, we have to be struck by its regularity. The natural world is full of systems, recurrent patterns, and scientific 'laws'. Many of us have learned these laws and systems in school, particularly in chemistry and physics. We learned Boyle's law about air pressure, Newton's laws of motion, the Periodic Table of the elements and so on. To the scientific mind, it is difficult to believe that there is a God who invented or created these physical laws, in the sense that he might have invented different laws. It is a temptation for us to see these laws as having priority even over God. We cannot imagine a universe in which the square on the hypotenuse is not equal to the square on the other two sides. It is then an easy step to believe that in his work of creation, God is determined or limited by a set of prior laws, so that he does not have complete freedom to do this or that. The scientific mind, if it is prepared to countenance the existence of God, demands at least that this God be a 'regular guy' who follows the rules and knows his place, rather like, as was said earlier, a giant impersonal computer. Apart from that he has no function.

But the God described in Christian revelation does not seem to be at all like the God that some of the scientists, such as Hawking, are prepared to accommodate in their system. Instead of an automaton or a computer, we find in the holy books a person with a very distinct and even 'quirky' personality. The Christian God is indeed a Prime Mover, but he is a Prime Mover With Idiosyncrasies. This can be a very scary thought, even for the non-scientist. It raises the kind of mind-blowing questions that many theologians, particularly Karl Barth, have debated – questions such as, Why is God this kind of God, and not some other kind of God? (Answer: Because God in his freedom has chosen this way of being); What determines the nature of God? (Answer: God). Barth concludes that God's way of living and loving is absolutely his own, in no way dictated to him from outside or conditioned by any higher necessity.

In so far as we can grasp this, it is a terrifying thought. Even in the cosmic myths that we construct ourselves, there is always implicitly some limiting factor to protect the universe from chaos. If there is a wicked witch, there is always a fairy godmother. We cannot accept the possibility that Superman will be ultimately vanquished by Lex Luthor. But there is no limiting factor where God is concerned except God himself. Still we may perhaps hope that God is a 'regular guy', the kind of God whose profile we could arrive at by logic and reason. But revelation suggests that this is a vain expectation. Barth does conclude that God 'cannot be other than he is'. Yet our question, What is God like?, cannot be answered by logic and reason. We have to take God as we find him, as revealed to us in the pages of our holy books. And the God we find is one who, among other things, has a distinct bias towards the poor and downtrodden.

*The Option for the Poor*
In some ways it is a pity that latter-day emphasis on the

option for the poor has an identifiable modern origin, namely the 1968 Medellin Conference and the 1971 Synod. For those who wished to take exception to it, it was too easy to say that it was a 'new-fangled' idea emanating from Marxist clerics. In fact, no message comes out louder from the gospels than the fact that God is biased in favour of the poor and the outsider. The fact that the bishops had to draw attention to this shows how successful the gospels of rationalism and economism had been in drowning out the Magnificat, the Sermon on the Mount, and most of the parables.

The truth is that God is defined by his option for the poor. It is not, of course, the only way of defining God, but it is the most important one. For particular historical reasons, the early theologians were much more concerned with defining the nature of God in quasi-philosophical categories, declaring that he was one being in three persons, and that he was almighty, with power that was not limited in any way. This philosophical approach had the effect of depersonalising God. For one thing, if God is thought of as 'perfect', it does not encourage us to look for distinguishing marks since, in our limited understanding, they may be seen as flaws. We might say of a human acquaintance, 'He was a very good man, but he was too kind to beggars', implying a personality defect. In human logic, as St Paul never tired of pointing out, God is full of such personality defects. In particular he is very biased towards poor people and, perhaps more alarmingly, very prejudiced against rich people ('It is easier for a camel to pass through the eye of a needle than for a rich man to enter the kingdom of heaven').

Although the scientist that is in all of us may find it difficult to cope with the idea of a Prime Mover With Idiosyncrasies, we may find belief in such a being more of a challenge, and something that can seriously engage us, than belief in a heavenly computer. People want, not just something to believe in, but somebody. They want faith, not just belief. A God that can be deduced through abstract formulae is unlikely to be ever anything more than something. The God of Christian revelation, especially as revealed in the person of Jesus Christ, is very much somebody. Such a God can also spur us to action, in a way that no abstract construct can. The option for the poor also brought with it the faith that does justice, because we cannot maintain our personal integrity if we declare our faith in God but fail to act in line with what that God clearly wants of us.

The option for the poor comes to us from revelation. However there is always a danger that it may become cut adrift from this revelation. Concern for the poor is, after all, a value in itself. Many people in the world who have no interest in God have opted for the poor. At the same time where the option for the poor comes adrift from the gospels and the church, it loses its roots, and the other foundations it attaches to may not be so secure. It does not have a 'rational' basis in what passes for rationality in much of our modern culture.

But there is another danger, which is perhaps more real for the church today. If, rather than the option for the poor losing touch with the church, the church instead drifts away from the option for the poor, an important part of revelation may be effectively lost to the church. The option for the poor, when it is operative in the life of the church, shows us what God is like. It reminds us that God, a real person, with a real, somewhat quirky personality, is a God who loves the underdog and the loser, a God we would be likely to find very annoying were he again to come down among us, a God we would never employ as a gardener. If we abandon the option for the poor we may find out that there is not much else, in our liturgy or in our theology, that presents to us a God who is distinctive and concrete, a God we might want to get to know rather than just know about.

# CHAPTER TWO

# A Relational God
## Some Reflections on The Trinity

*Aileen Walsh*

The God question is a crucial one. How we understand the mystery that permeates and surrounds us and our world is key because it acts as an ultimate reference point for understanding ourselves, our experience, life and the world. What we really believe in deeply effects and directs how we behave, what we value, the way we live our lives and what type of society we create. The God question I believe is a particularly urgent one today. We are living in a world of growing disillusionment with institutional religion. Many people have let go of their belief in God but remain hungry and searching. There are many indications in our society that the loss experienced by vast numbers of people leaves a deep vacuum yet to be filled.

In a recent volume of essays, which explores the most important spiritual questions for our time, Sandra Schneiders makes this same point. 'Is there a God?' she asks, 'and if so what is God like?' She goes on to say that this question is not just a theoretical issue to occupy the minds of underemployed academics but is a really crucial one since – 'Who God really is determines what we, made in God's image and likeness, are called to become.'[1] – So the God question is also a question about ourselves.

The doctrine of the Trinity is the specifically Christian way of speaking about God. The *Catechism* describes this doctrine as the 'central mystery of the Christian faith and

---

1. Schneiders Sandra M., 'God is the Question and God is the Answer' in *Spiritual Questions for the 21st Century*, Editor Snyder Mary Hembrow, Orbis Books, Maryknoll, New York 2001.

life', yet curiously enough this doctrine is rather remote from people's everyday experience. For most of us Christians the reality of the indwelling Trinity is lightly dismissed as a mystery beyond our knowledge and understanding, having no practical impact on our daily lives. It is often regarded as just an article of faith we vaguely ascribe to, but with no real relationship to life. Not only that, apparently the great dread of the preacher is the Trinity Sunday sermon. The result of this is that trinitarian theology, which is abundantly fertile ground for reflection on every dimension of Christian life, is often neglected by preachers or made to appear distant, utterly abstract or contrary to reason.

I reflected on all of this a couple of years ago on Trinity Sunday as I walked in the Dublin mini marathon. The profound and moving experience of being alongside 30,000 women all wearing t-shirts representing different charities, was made more profound when, as we passed Holles St Maternity Hospital, someone held up a new born baby at a window and from the crowd of women as we passed underneath there was a chorus of sighs. I was overcome with the experience of God's presence in our midst. I felt – this is it; this is the heart of the mystery of the Trinity. I felt immersed in God's love. I was conscious of God's life flowing in and through community. I had a sense of warmth and connectedness, people reaching out of themselves and living for others, people rooted in some ultimate unity, all heightened in the presence of new life. In a world often characterised by alienation, loneliness, greed, selfishness, individualism and excessive competitiveness, this was certainly the opposite feeling.

How do we know about the mystery of the Trinity anyway? Jesus didn't call the disciples aside and say, 'By the way there is just one more thing you should know – in God there are three divine persons and yet only one God.' There is indeed no formal doctrine of the Trinity in the New Testament. The only reason we know about the

Trinity is because the first disciples experienced God relating to them in this dynamic threefold way. How they expressed this experience was to say that they were saved by God, through Christ, in the power of the Holy Spirit. The doctrine of the Trinity was a much later reflection on the written account of this experience. The central point was and is that the disciples experienced God as a *relating* God who engaged them in a relationship of love and transformation. In Jesus they experienced God and were utterly changed by the encounter. The New Testament is an attempt to be faithful to all the dimensions of that experience. It was the task of later theology to reflect on their experiences.

The doctrine of the Trinity is a theological construct which attempts to put words on the liberating God encountered in history. In the early days of the church's life Christians reflected deeply on the meaning of their lives in the light of Christ's revelation. Their self-understanding grew alongside their understanding of plurality in God. Gradually this position was formulated and reached a certain sense of clarity in the Council of Nicea (325 CE). At that point there was a great deal of vitality surrounding the issue. The nature of God was vital to people's lives. When the doctrine was crystallised in the Scholastic formulation it appeared more like a problem to be tidied up to the satisfaction of the thinking mind. Trinity as a doctrine was beautifully and neatly parcelled in metaphysically accurate terminology but it lost its relevance to people's everyday lives. There is an urgent need for us today to recover and retrieve the sense of meaning and vitality at the heart of the doctrine, which is ultimately a practical doctrine with radical consequences for Christian life.

The heart of the trinitarian theology is a theology of relationship, God to us, we to God, we to each other and all creation. The doctrine summarises what it means to participate in the life of God, through Jesus in the Spirit. The mystery of God is revealed in Christ and the Spirit as the mystery of love. It reveals that there is only one God and God's being by nature is relational. This is also our nature. Jesus Christ came to give us the most important truth upon which all of reality is founded. He came to teach us that we are unique persons, not by being an isolated individual but by being in vital, loving and personal relationships with another. God moves towards us so that we may move towards each other and, thereby, towards God.

Trinitarian theology puts priority on relationships, communion, reciprocity and connection. God as Trinity expresses not only mutuality of relation between persons, but also their distinctiveness and diversity and the need to respect this. It points to the fact that the only value of ultimate significance in our lives is relationships. Every relationship is a sacred encounter. As a counsellor, I listen to people's stories all the time. I am intensely aware of the challenge of relationships. It is the place where people experience vulnerability and pain but also joy and fulfilment. It is beautiful and disarming to see a young baby smiling back so readily in response to a smile – it touches the heart. But as the baby grows up through childhood, adolescence and adulthood, barriers are put up; people gather baggage and relationships become more guarded, difficult and complicated. The challenge of our lives is to live in a community with a strong, healthy sense of ourselves and at the same time being truly open to the other and all others in our community.

The mystery of the Trinity draws attention to the challenge at the heart of living community, to live the trinitarian life of unity in diversity. The real challenge is not just relating to the other but to all others, wherever they are encountered – to live our lives based on a belief in the fundamental equality of each and every person. We all have a part to play in the final story. So then, to be in the image of God is to be in community – a community that is not just an amorphous mass of people, but a community that respects a radical equality and the distinctiveness of each individual.

The heart of trinitarian theology is that of right relationship. Clearly then the doctrine of the Trinity is a practical doctrine which challenges every aspect of how we live our lives, and manage our relationships, personally, nationally and internationally, but its scope is even broader than that. Today many conversations between science and theology have highlighted the cosmic significance of the mystery of the Trinity. We have become conscious that the world in which we live is a vast network of web-like relationships, of interconnectedness and interdependence which, because of the way we have abused it, is threatened with ecological disaster. There is then a global dimension to the challenge.

While the doctrine of the Trinity doesn't give us a clear blueprint to follow in managing our relationships and institutions it does give us the ideals to aim for. We can look at some practical examples of the challenges to live Trinitarian faith:

• God has made us all different. Difference is 'of' God. We each have our particular part to play in our society. It is the responsibility of each of us to turn away from divisiveness and move towards community – building a community that respects difference. We need to let go of the 'isms' that plague humanity whether they are based on race, gender, class, sexual orientation or religious creed.

• There is an urgent need for us today in Ireland to challenge our exam points system which has at its core an individualism which favours the materially well off and the bright. The powerful message this conveys to each new generation is contributing to the creation of a self-centred, elite and divided society. Those who do not succeed or opt out are left with a sense of failure that they have nothing to contribute to society. Can we honestly say that our educational system fosters a society with equal opportunity for all?

- While the trinitarian doctrine of God might not specify the exact forms of structure and community appropriate to the church, it does provide the critical principle against which we can measure present institutional arrangements. We can just ask whether our institutional rituals and administrative practice foster elitism, discrimination, competition or any of the other 'isms', or whether the church reflects the relational nature of God, i.e. a domain of inclusiveness, interdependence and cooperation among equals. There are some breathtaking disparities. The marginalisation of women is one obvious example where the Spirit is actively engaged in redressing the balance.

- The effects of globalisation, defined as the integration of the economies of the world, has really resulted in an economic imperialism. It has widened the gap between the rich and the poor of our world, placing the power and benefit in the hands of the upper 15%. It has no respect for the uniqueness of people's culture. Decision-making is left in the hands of a few, decisions that effect the entire population of the world. The impact of all this is an excluded majority who slip further into poverty. Trinitarian faith means we have to question this trend towards globalisation and work for the restoration of justice and harmony in all the relationships of the world.

- Over the last number of years we have become more and more aware of the degree to which our selfish and exploitative behaviour has wreaked havoc in the natural world. We are engaged in a rampant destruction and poisoning of our environment. Today chemical and nuclear industries have the power to scar the earth, poisoning the water, air and soil, killing off many life forms and threatening the safety of our entire planet.

Reflection on the results of all this has made us conscious that the world in which we live is a vast network of web-like relationships, of interconnectedness and interdependence. Living trinitarian faith challenges us to care for the earth, to work to restore the balance and reverence it as God's creation.

So believing in a Trinitarian God is not at all remote from everyday life. It is hoping for a different kind of society, one where connections and relations are treated with reverence but where the tensions of difference and otherness challenge the limits of our structures, laws and traditions.

I introduced this chapter by making the point that the God question is a crucial one because how we image God effects how we live our lives. So what then, we may ask, is the image of God we live out of today? I think we are actually in a state of flux and transition of shifting consciousness. There is a degree to which our image of God is changing and the changes taking place would suggest a move towards a trinitarian relational image of God. In saying this I am making no claim that people are aware of the shift. In fact it is very difficult to know to what degree at any point in time people are aware of the image of God they live out of.

We are living in an era of remarkable social changes. Structures are breaking down in all areas of society. Our times have been described as pluralist and secularised. We see on the one hand people who attend church on a regular basis but who appear not to relate this practice to their daily living. On the other hand we have many individuals and groups who are passionately concerned with issues of poverty, justice, discrimination and the care of the environment, some of whom relate their stance to an image of God, but others who very definitely want God left out of it. Today there is great interest in meditation and all forms of contemplative prayer. Some of this is being explored within the Christian mystical and contemplative tradition, but many have gone towards the east in their hunger and search for a new wisdom to inform their living. The experience of many Christians is that there is an absence of wisdom in how we relate to ourselves, the rest of humanity and the environment. They are searching for spiritual sources to nourish and guide their hearts and minds to new and better ways of living.

Maybe we can say that in searching for the solutions to the problems of society we are unconsciously reaching towards a trinitarian awareness of God – a paradigm of reality that is relational and that works. One way or the other we are in the process today of shedding images of God that have defined our self-understanding for the past millennium. In general, before Vatican II, the image of God which people had was authoritarian and fatherly and this informed our living and spirituality. The heart of the theology, which characterises the shift in Vatican II, is the retrieval of the God who is love, the God who is relational and engages each one of us in a relationship of love, the God who is Father, Son and Holy Spirit.

Until relatively recently there was a neglect of the third person of the Blessed Trinity. While we were quite clear on the first and second persons, Father and Son, the Holy Spirit seemed to represent for people a shadowy figure who hovered vaguely around somewhere. (The use of exclusively male imagery for the first and second persons had a further limiting effect but that would have to be the subject matter of another paper.)

Because of the neglect of the Holy Spirit we lost sight of the divine presence within us, the dynamic energy of God calling us to right relationship. What has been neglected in the forgetfulness around the Spirit has been nothing less than God's ongoing relationship with the world. There are many indications today of a shift in our awareness of God who is nearer to us than we are to ourselves. We listen to the signs of the times because we trust that the Holy Spirit is speaking through these. We recognise that the Spirit is alive and active in the many voices (often from the margins) calling out for change in the church and in society as a whole. These are the prophets of today who, like Jeremiah of the Old Testament, speak out because of the fire that burns within. The present upsurge of interest in the mystical and contemplative traditions is, I believe, a further indication of a recovery in the awareness of God who is within us.

So we are today more in touch with the God who is relationship, yet speech about God is always difficult; God is ultimate mystery. Language used in this context is only analogous and yet it really does matter because the image of God we have acts as the ultimate reference point for the values of a community. The doctrine of the Trinity in the past has often appeared like a mathematical puzzle rather than what it is, a metaphor to put words on the God encountered in history. Revitalising the richness of the Triune symbol requires that we first of all strip the language of its literalness and delve underneath to the richness it reveals. When we do this we can see that the heart of the doctrine points to the relational nature of God which is also our nature.

Having said all of that it is worth remembering the first disciples were not transformed by their knowledge of the doctrine of the Trinity but by the encounter with God — Father, Son and Holy Spirit. So it is not surprising that the real prophets of today are often those who are the mystics and contemplatives. The heart of true mysticism now, as always, is the encounter with God deep within, who invites us out of our individualistic, self-centred ways to build a community of equals, and a world of harmony in relatedness. In a world characterised by so much evil and injustice, an encounter with the God who is love cannot but disturb, a disturbance which is the energy of God, inviting us, leading us, challenging us, empowering us to live God's life, to be who we are called to be.

# CHAPTER THREE

# Unripened Fruits

## *Jim Corkery SJ*

This chapter is about unripened fruits: things in Christianity that are capable of nourishing the world in new and unexpected ways, if only they were allowed to flourish. The trouble is, fruits like these are often kept in the dark; and people sometimes even conspire to keep them hidden. About fifty years ago, there was a French professor of theology, a man named Henri de Lubac, whose daring ideas about God's closeness to the human world – and the human world's fundamental closeness to God – led to his being silenced by the Vatican for a while. It was a painful time for de Lubac, yet he used it positively. For ten years he devoted himself to the study of Buddhism, after which he said that it was the greatest spiritual fact outside of Christianity. This was a rather appreciative statement for those times, when the dialogue between the religions was not favoured in the way that it is today. It was in de Lubac's daring to look deeply into a religion with which he was not familiar that he discovered riches beyond all possible imagining – and a radical programme that enriched, and challenged, his own Christianity.

For most of us, not only in unfamiliar religions but even within our own, there are riches that lie undiscovered: unripened fruits that, if they matured, could really nourish our broken world. In relation to Christianity, Christians are often a bit like de Lubac had been in relation to Buddhism: unaware of the richness it contains. Thus Christians miss all sorts of things that lie hidden within their religion. Part of this is due to the blinkered education they received. For example, when I was a child I learned the mysteries of the rosary: the joyful, the sorrowful and the glorious mysteries. I never noticed then that they dealt only with the very early life of Jesus, and after that with his death and resurrection, but not at all with his adult life and ministry: his preaching, healing and consoling; his prophetic teaching. All of these are vividly portrayed in the gospels, in which Jesus is depicted as untiringly preaching the kingdom of God. Yet it was only later in my life, on receiving an opportunity to look more deeply into the gospels, that I saw that a lot had been left out in the Jesus I was taught about. 'Gentle Jesus, meek and mild', yes, I had caught that – and the fact that I was supposed to act like him myself, everywhere. But prophetic, denouncing, questioning Jesus – what about being like him? I had heard nothing at all about this Jesus, and about the turbulence that imitation of him might involve. So, there remained unripened fruits.

I wonder how it was with you, the reader of this page? Did you, when you grew up, discover riches within your Christianity that were hidden from you as a child? Or were you left to manage with the heritage of those early years only? In the last thirty years or so, Christians (first in Latin America and then more widely) discovered many of the (as yet) unripened fruits in Christianity that could lead to the gospel revolutionising the lives of poor people. And it was the same with regard to women, who for so long were kept on the margins of social and, indeed, of church life. Women began to discover that the same gospel which had, unfortunately, been used to keep them 'in their place', also contained the seeds of their liberation and their inclusion in new places. Perhaps you have not yet had this experience of discovering unripened gospel fruits, but maybe you would like to? If you would, read on. If, however, you wish to continue undisturbed (and undisturbing!), then we should probably part company at this point …

*Seeing things in a new way*

Ah, you're still there! Alright then, I presume you are
ready to journey further with me. Well, the first thing that
is necessary is a shift in perspective: a shift from an indi-
vidual-centred to a more socially-centred viewpoint. In the
past, undoubtedly, some truly valuable things were em-
phasised: that God loved me; that every single person was
of infinite value in God's eyes; that every Christian standing in a relationship of friendship with God was a 'temple
of the Holy Spirit' and that this Holy Spirit lived in his or
her heart; that to be a Christian was to know oneself called,
loved, intended and chosen by God from all time and for
all time (H. U. von Balthasar). These were – indeed are –
valuable and eternal truths, but they are all focused on the
individual and on his/her essentially private relationship
with God. They say little about finding God in our relationships, not even in our one-to-one (or micro) relationships, and certainly not in our community (or macro) relationships.

Here lies an unripened fruit: the insight that relationship with God is not just a matter of God and me, but also
a matter of God and you-and-me and, even more so, of
God and us. Here is a point neglected in traditional spirituality, namely, that being close to God – being in communion with God – is directly bound up with being close to
others, being in communion with them. Instead of the
'God-me' relationship being seen as a 'removed', separate-
from-the-world, cocooned existence, it is seen to involve
communion both with my close others (in the micro-relational spheres of family, friendship, etc.) and with my
more distant others (in the macro-relational spheres of
workplace, locality, city, nation, international community,
etc.). A fruit has ripened here: God is seen as being found
not in flight from others and from the world, but rather in
flight to others and to the world. And as this fruit is further
peeled today, it is seen that God is found in a special way

through relationship with those others who are different from me – in race, creed, gender, etc. – and even more so in those who are excluded from the life of the community, because God as revealed in Jesus is one who goes after the other and the excluded and, as we do likewise, we discover God already there before us – in their faces, revealing God's own face.

Being close to God, in the perspective just outlined, remains distinct from closeness to others; but it is never separate from it. In this perspective, the way to God is through others and being with others is the way to God. God's face is found in others' faces: not just in family and friends either, but particularly in those faces that society tries to hide and shout down, like the blind beggar, Bartimaeus, was shouted down in the gospel – shouted down, indeed, by those who considered themselves the followers of Jesus – so that Jesus had to go to the edge (the margin – note the symbolism) and explicitly give a hearing to the one that everyone else was ignoring. Unripened fruit here, is there not? And not one that will be found by merely examining one's personal relationship with God. It will be found only by examining one's context, one's situation, one's surrounding world. Looking at Jesus means looking around, not just looking up. The figure on the cross stretches not only up to the Father but out to the world. Even for Jesus, the way to his Father was through love for his sisters and brothers.

*Beyond 'God-and-me'*
One of the reasons that the 'God and me' emphasis was very strong was the focus, in teaching and in moral theology, on sin and guilt in each individual's life, which had to be sorted out with God alone, mainly in the sacrament of confession. It is true that there was always a 'reconciliation-with-the-community' aspect to this sacrament; but it was scarcely visible. Sometimes the element of 'God and you-

and-me' surfaced, as, for example, in a case of two people in a family fighting, or two friends refusing to reconcile with each other. Then it was seen that coming back to a right relationship with God – again mainly through con-fession – meant that you had to go and try to make up with the other person and say sorry for whatever you had done wrong. However, it was not really made clear that that other person, far from being a potential obstacle in your relationship with God, might more likely be a channel for relationship with God. We should have been able to see this, not least because of the very rich understanding of marriage coming out of the Second Vatican Council. Such an understanding could have communicated that another person is my way to God, my principal path to God, God's main way of being lovingly present to me, so that we to-gether, in fact, could better grow closer to God than I alone. Some people, the more poetic and artistic perhaps, came to see that: 'to love another person is to see the face of God' (*Les Miserables*). But the theologians and the catech-ists did not teach this idea very much – maybe they did not even notice it – and while they did come, in time, to speak of relationship with God being like relationship with some loved other person, they did not really speak of that other being one's ordinary, everyday path to God: one's regular way of meeting God in the world.

You can see there was some improvement in the way things were seen, as close others (spouses, friends) were brought into the picture a bit more. Yet there remained a lack. For it was still possible to exclude the truly 'other' under that viewpoint. Family, friends, relatives – yes, they had a claim to attention and they had a significance in terms of how God is present to us. But what of the reli-giously, politically, racially other, not to mention those of the other gender? The perspective just outlined said noth-ing about meeting God in and through meeting them. So a 'you scratch my back and I'll scratch yours' kind of mentality, a kind of 'old boys network', could prevail. The problem is (and the gospel has pointed this out too) you find this kind of clique-making everywhere. And so the radical implications of Christianity for relationships with those who are truly other remained another unripened fruit in this very limited perspective.

*Beyond 'God and you-and-me'*
Now if, focusing on the micro-relational or one-to-one sphere, it was difficult to get across how the (similarly) other was a path to God – and almost impossible to convey the significance of the truly other, then imagine how hard it was to see the community and God as being in relationship. Communities, social groups, collectivities could not possibly relate to God as a whole, could they? Surely that was only for individuals, ultimately? Funny question, that, since most believers notice quickly enough that 'no one can be a Christian in isolation' (Joseph Ratzinger) and that faith is a matter of piggybacking: I on your faith (when mine is shaky); you on mine (when it is vice versa); and, above all, you and me on our faith, the community's faith, the faith of the people of God to which we belong. And yet, the communal or 'we' character of faith (and grace – God's presence) was obscured.

Given the blindness that I have just described, you can imagine how long it took me to see that the together of Christianity meant far more, was far richer even, than simply the together of the one-to-one relationship. There were things I feel I should have seen, but I just did not notice them and, as with the mysteries of the rosary, nobody else was drawing attention to what had been left out either. For example, we were taught lovely things about being made in the image and likeness of God, but here God was always thought of in God's oneness/singularity and the human being was always seen simply as an individual. But what about the truth that the Christian God is in fact

One-and-Three, Three-in-One, that is, Trinity: a three-per-soned God? And if human beings are made in the image of this God, the only God Christianity knows, Three-in-One, One-in-Three, then are not people together as much, indeed in a sense more an image of God than persons on their own? For God is never, from all eternity, an alone-standing God. As theologians say nowadays: God is community-in-unity, unity-in-community (Enda Mc Donagh). And are not we the same, or at least meant to be, called to be, the same: community-in-unity and unity-in-community: humanity all together imaging the kaleidoscopic colourfulness and plurality of God: image of the Trinity – so that you could say we are never more like God than when together, never less like God than when apart? Just think of the picture of all the nations together at the opening of the Olympic Games: does humanity like this not image much more richly the splendid diversity of the one, unified, three-personed God?

Now where is the isolated individual in the Christian picture? Still there, to be sure, and there in dignity and splendour also; but no longer the entire picture, as if the group and the community were secondary. The individual and the community are really correlative – with the community being, in a definite sense, prior (Bernard Lonergan) – but this primacy of community was lost on me growing up because of how we were taught, even though Christianity had always contained the unripened fruits that testified to the centrality of human togetherness. Where were these unripened fruits, then, these hints of this central togetherness? In the eucharist, for example; and in the Christian doctrine of grace.

First, the eucharist. We actually call it communion, which means being-together. Yet we did not learn about it as a together thing. Instead we learned to receive an individual host (not a piece of bread broken from the bread consecrated at the altar) and we learned to return to our seats reverently, hunkering down into a very private thanksgiving between me and the God I had received, but failing to notice that being in communion with this God meant being in communion with the people round about also. Those people, those other Christian believers/receivers, together with me, became the Body of Christ that we received in that, on eating the eucharistic bread, we became part of what we ate rather than, as is normally the case, what we ate became part of us (St Augustine). So you see: we spoke of going to communion, not seeing that it meant, indeed it fashioned, expressed, necessitated, our togetherness, our being in communion as members of the one Body of Christ (Juan Luis Segundo). This being in communion with God and one another is grace, God's life in us.

*Grace: the Trinitarian God, Father, Son, Spirit, living and active in world history*
The word 'grace' refers to the presence of the trinitarian God in us and in the world, making it (creation), healing it (redemption) and drawing it closer to themselves (sanctification). Grace is 'God-with-us'. And to be with us more intimately, God 'left home', as it were, the Son becoming human – one with all of humanity – and the Spirit becoming Life itself, the divine life indwelling the entire world. What the Son did touched all; what the Spirit does enlivens all. Our traditional understandings of the activities of these two divine Persons situated them, basically, in the bodies and souls of individuals. But now, with an enriched social perspective, we see that they inhabit society, culture, history, the cosmos. The cosmos, yes. Look at Jesus. No longer, now, would we simply speak of God becoming human in him at a particular point in time, important as this was. Rather we would begin with something like the Letter to Ephesians, speaking of God's plan for the whole world, hidden for ages (although at work) and finally re-

vealed in a spectacularly visible way through what God
did in Jesus. We would see, then, that God's work in Jesus
was cosmic in dimensions: intended to transform the
whole of human history, the whole universe, through a
unique event within that universe. As Pope John Paul II
said recently: 'Faith in Christ who became incarnate in history does not only transform individuals inwardly, but
also regenerates peoples and their cultures.' In other
words, Christ is not just for the salvation of each – in a private 'Jesus-me' relationship. He draws people together,
welding them into community (his body) and transform-
ing social life round about him. It is not just individuals
who bear the traces of Christ. It was Saint Augustine who
wrote: 'The whole of history is pregnant with Christ.' In
other words, it is not only individuals, but the whole of
human history, the whole world, that is being transformed
by Christ's incarnate presence. Cultures and societies, and
not just individuals, bear the traces (the 'footprints') of
Jesus Christ. He is to be found enfleshed in them; he wants
to become enfleshed in them; he can be expected to be
traced in them; his incarnation is inculturation. Christian
faith's vision is, in short, that his traces/footprints are
there. All we have to do is to be detectives of these (already
present) traces – detectives, that is, who are sophisticated
seers, a bit like modern bomb-disposal experts, aware that
what we find will be dangerous, transformative, socially
explosive.

The Christian understanding of the Spirit has had a
similar social development. The action of the Spirit is not
confined simply to indwelling the hearts of individual
Christians, as we used to think, or even to indwelling the
Christian community, the church. Again it is John Paul II
who said: 'Our gaze now extends to the horizons of the
world and the whole of human history ... It is impossible
for us to limit ourselves to the 2,000 years which have
passed since the birth of Jesus Christ. Indeed, we "need to

go further back, to embrace the whole of the action of the Holy Spirit even before Christ – from the beginning, throughout the world, and especially in the economy of the Old Covenant" (*Dominum et Vivificantem*, n. 53b).' He adds: 'There is no corner of creation and no moment of history in which the Spirit is not at work.' Nor is it the case – and this is true both of Jesus Christ and of the Holy Spirit – that their presence is confined to what we would call salvation history; no, it runs through the entire history of the world, seeking to burst out everywhere. And it is the job of the church, the community of believers, to highlight, foster, embrace the ubiquitous presence of God's Spirit.

All of this is what Christians have always called grace, the deepest meaning of which always refers in some way to the experience of the presence of God in our world. That experience has been highlighted a little in the foregoing, as we have examined how the Creator, Christ and the Spirit are the Triune God being present in our world, present as 'God-with-us' (grace). But how do we see, trace, their presence? 'Eyes' are needed for that, are they not? And given what we have been saying, two questions arise: where should we be looking, and how should we be looking? We should be looking out, around, up ahead – at society, history, the earth, the cosmos. And we should be looking together; for together we image better, far better, far more accurately, the very God we seek to uncover.

## Concluding remarks

We have to stop here, more on a threshold than at a destination. I have lately been reading a new novel called *The Lovely Bones*. All of human life is there and, like many a good novel, you cannot read it without becoming aware of what Saint Augustine once articulated: 'I am human, and nothing human is alien from me.' I thought all the good thoughts and felt all the good feelings of the book's characters; but I thought and felt many of the evil ones too –

not that I had the murderer's intent, but so evil were his actions that murder was my intent towards him. It struck me, in this maelstrom of what is humanly good and humanly evil, that on our own – the murderer was an isolate – we cannot hope to do the good, love the beautiful, know the true, at least in a right and accountable way that acknowledges our responsibilities towards one another as members of a human community and maybe, within that, of a religious family. So it is a matter of reaching out to touch, not of drawing back in secret. It used to be said: 'God is not in the commotion'; I would rather say that, for us human beings, 'God is not in the isolation'. Isolation is not the same thing as being alone, of course; it is more about the single 'patch' pulling away from the 'quilt' of humanity-together. This destroys the patch – and it mars the quilt too. Surely there is an important lesson there.

# CHAPTER FOUR

# Mary's Vision of Justice outlined in the *Magnificat*

*Peter McVerry SJ*

Sometimes my faith grows dim. Sometimes I wonder is there a God at all or are we all just fooling ourselves. Why did God make it so difficult for us to believe in God if it is so important? Could God not do a little parting of the Liffey waters from time to time, just to prove that God exists – though you still wouldn't be able to walk across with the dirt you'd find there! I resonate with the authorities in Israel who, when Jesus came and said that he was from God and had a revelation from God, asked him to give them a sign that he was who he said he was. 'If you are the Son of God tell this stone to turn into a loaf' (Luke 4:3). And again, 'If you are the Son of God, throw yourself down from this tower' (Luke 4:9). And what does Jesus say? 'No sign shall be given to this generation' (Mark 8:12). I always thought that that was most unreasonable of him – the least he could do was to give them a little sign.

In fact, Jesus was giving signs all the time, but they couldn't read them. One person asked for a sign and got it. That was John the Baptist. John, from his prison cell, sent his messengers to Jesus with the question: 'Are you the one who is to come or have we got to wait for someone else?' (Matthew 11:3). In other words, give us a sign. And what does Jesus say? 'Go back and tell John what you hear and see: the blind see again, and the lame walk, lepers are cleansed and the deaf hear and the dead are raised to life and the Good News is proclaimed to the poor; and happy the man who does not lose faith in me' (Matthew 11:4–6). In other words, the signs that Jesus was from God were the signs of compassion. Jesus was trying to say: 'Miracles prove nothing – every generation has its magicians! But if you knew who God was, if you knew that our God is a God of compassion, then you would recognise that I am from God by the signs of compassion that I do. If you do not recognise that I am from God, then you do not know God.' We look at a child in the pram and we say: 'Oh, he's lovely, he's the image of his father/mother.' So Jesus was trying to say: 'The only way to know whether I have come from God is if you see in me the same likeness that you find in the Father.' Our God is a God of compassion and the only way we can recognise the Son of God is through the Son's compassion.

So when my faith grows dim, where do I go to have my faith restored? Moving statues? Forget it. What sort of God would have even the remotest interest in playing games with statues? When my faith grows dim, my faith is restored by the countless acts of compassion of innumerable people who are reaching out to the sick, to the lonely, to the poor and the marginalised, to the dying and the unwanted. There I find evidence that God exists.

Of course this is not evidence in the scientific sense of the word. I cannot prove that God exists, neither to anyone else, nor even to myself. But what I can do is to confirm, in my own experience, that I am loved, infinitely and unconditionally, by a being I call God.

I am loved infinitely: God wishes me to be happy. There is no happiness that God withholds from me. God desires my infinite happiness. And so I am loved infinitely. It is this love that gives me my value. I am like a Picasso painting: a Picasso painting, valued at £50m, where does its value come from? It comes from outside itself. Its value is given to it. It is valued at £50m because others give it that value, others love it to that extent. But although its value comes from outside itself, its value resides in the painting itself. If I put an exact, identical copy of the painting beside it, the copy has little or no value. The value is in the Picasso painting but the value is given to it from outside itself. And so my value comes from outside myself, from the infinite love of God for me. And so I am of infinite value. I have this unsurpassable dignity, which has been given to me.

I am loved unconditionally. Nothing can separate me from the love of God. The one thing in this world that never changes is God's love. And so no one, nothing, not even my own sinfulness, can take away, or reduce, the value and dignity that God's love bestows on me. Being loved infinitely and unconditionally gives me an infinite dignity and value that can never be taken from me.

This conviction that I am loved infinitely and unconditionally is the foundation stone of justice. If I can confirm that I am loved infinitely and unconditionally, then so can everyone else. If I have this infinite dignity, then so has everyone else. This conviction is a challenge to our culture, which seeks to give value to people by what they do, what they achieve, how they succeed. Our culture seeks to value people by what comes out of them; our faith seeks to value people by the love of God, which has been put into them.

## Link between Faith and Justice

For me the link between faith and justice is this dignity of people. We could sum up the whole gospel by saying that Jesus came to proclaim that God is the Father of every human being; and conversely that every human being is a child of God and has the dignity of being a child of God.

But if our faith proclaims in words the dignity of every human being, then our commitment to justice seeks to make that dignity a reality for every human being. Faith without justice is hypocrisy – it is empty words that mean nothing because we have taken the meaning out of them. Justice seeks to put that meaning back into the words, to make reality reflect what we say, and what we say to reflect reality.

And so compassion is the heart and soul of justice; it is the beginning, the middle and the end of our commitment to justice. Our reaching out to those whose dignity is being denied or threatened by the way in which they are treated by society is the meaning and the content of our struggle for justice.

*Motivation for our commitment to justice*
Why do I commit myself to this reaching out, which can be difficult, self-sacrificing and problematic? Is it for the sake of the reward, the Kingdom of God, which is promised to those who reach out to the poor? No. Is it for fear of punishment, if I fail to show love? No. The motivation for our commitment to justice is gratitude, gratitude for the infinite and unconditional love which God has given to me. The deeper my appreciation of that love, the greater my gratitude and the greater my commitment to justice can be. So the foundation stone for justice is my appreciation of that love of God.

So the first half of the *Magnificat* speaks to me of Mary's total conviction, borne from her own experience, of the love of God for her, freely given, not deserved, and given in all the abundance which God is able to give. Mary is rooted in that deep appreciation of the dignity and value which she has been given by the love of God. She expresses her deep gratitude to God for that love.

In the second half of the *Magnificat*, Mary recognises that that same love, which has been poured out on her, moves God to reach out, in a special way, to the poor and the powerless.

### COMMITMENT TO JUSTICE

*1. A preferential option for the poor and powerless*
An image of God, which I often use, is this: Imagine a parent with two children: one of the children is doing her homework. She asks the parent to help her with her home-

work. So the parent goes over to help the child with the homework. While he is doing that, he looks out the window and sees their other child being beaten up outside. So what does he do? Well, obviously he leaves the child doing the homework and goes to the aid of the child being beaten up. Why does he do so? It is not because he loves the child being beaten up more than he loves the child doing the homework. No, he loves both children equally. But he leaves one child and goes to the aid of the other because of the situation that that child is in. The child is in a situation of danger, of pain, and so has a priority call on the parent's care and concern at that moment of time, which the other child does not require.

As I imagine God looking down at our world, God sees me writing to you and loves me with an infinite and unconditional love. I cannot ask for more than that. But God is also looking down on some poor mother in Sudan whose children are dying from hunger in her arms, or some homeless child in Dublin or London or Calcutta wondering where they are going to eat and sleep tonight, or some young mother waiting in her flat for her alcoholic husband to come in and wondering if he is going to beat her up again tonight. I would have to say, that if they did not have a priority concern for God, in a way that I do not require at this point in time, then God would not be a parent.

God's preferential option for the poor and the powerless comes, not from loving the poor and powerless more than the rest of us, but because God is compassion. The God who is compassion must have a special concern and care for those children who are suffering, who are in danger or in pain.

In a world of injustice, must we take sides? Yes, because God is compassion. To be for the poor and the powerless is not to be against anyone; it is to be *for*, for the poor and powerless, and to be an invitation to others to also be for

the poor and powerless, an invitation which of course they
may reject.

When Jesus was asked who would be in the kingdom of
God, he answered: 'How happy are you who are poor;
yours is the kingdom of God.' In school, I was taught that
at the last judgement, I would have to stand up on the plat-
form and all my sins would be revealed, and all the good
things I did would be revealed, and the weighing scales
would come out and maybe I would get in, or maybe not.
Then, after me, some other poor soul would have to get
up, and so on. Well, after the first few hundred thousand it
is going to get very boring! So maybe the last judgement
scene is not about the revelation of McVerry or anyone else
to the world. Maybe it is God's final revelation of who God
is to the world. Here we have the whole world gathered
before God and God finally reveals who God is. And who
is our God? Our God is compassion. And how better could
God reveal that God is compassion than to usher into the
kingdom all those who were made to suffer here on earth,
whose dignity was taken away from them, who were unwanted and rejected. The kingdom belongs to the poor. So
I am left watching the poor being given the kingdom, and
wondering do I get in or not! Well, I get in, if I have made
friends with the poor. If through my compassion, I have
made friends with the poor, then they will welcome me
into the kingdom, which they have been given. However,
if I have ignored them, failed to reach out to them, despised them, how can I then expect them to invite me into
their kingdom?

In our reaching out to the poor and our attempts to take
some of the suffering from their shoulders, nothing is un-
touchable, nothing is sacred. Some of the suffering, the
poverty and marginalisation that is imposed on many in
our world, is due to political failure, political policies and
decisions. There is a debate in many of the churches about
whether the church should get involved in politics. Many

would say it is no business of the church to meddle in politics, it knows nothing about politics and should stick to
what it is supposed to do – bring people to know God and
teach them to pray. But the church proclaims the dignity of
all people and where that dignity is undermined, threatened or taken away, then no area of human life is exempt
from the church's criticism and efforts to bring about
change, no door is closed to the church's prophetic call for
justice. If political decisions, policies or programmes im-
pose suffering and marginalisation on people and take
away the dignity that is theirs by right, then such decisions, policies or programmes must be challenged.

Another image I often use is of a fellow lying by a river
on a lovely sunny day. He is enjoying the peace and feeling
very contented. Suddenly, he sees a body floating down
the river. So he jumps in, pulls the body out, gives it the
kiss of life and sends the person on his way. He settles back
to enjoy the rest of the day, feeling very satisfied with himself, when another body comes floating down the river. So
he jumps in, pulls the body out, gives it the kiss of life and
sends her on her way. And a third body and a fourth, the
bodies just keep coming. At some point, he has to say to
himself, 'I must go up river and see where all the bodies
are coming from.' So up he goes and finds a bridge where
an oil tanker has crashed, spilt its oil on the bridge and
broken the side of the bridge. Everybody crossing the
bridge slips on the oil and falls into the river. So, he cleans
up the oil and puts a rope along the side of the bridge and
there are no more bodies floating down the river.

In our compassion for the poor and the powerless, we
must not only pull the bodies out of the river, but we must
go up river and fix the bridge. It is still important to pull
the bodies out of the river – the poor fellow floating down
the river doesn't want you to fix the bridge until after you
have rescued him out of the river. But we cannot be content with just pulling the bodies out of the river. At some

point we must also fix the bridge. Fixing the bridge may involve toppling princes – I think of President Marcos in the Philippines or Papa Doc Duvalier in Haiti. There may be smaller princes to be challenged, if Bertie and Charlie don't mind me calling them that, and toes to be trod upon! If some do not want the oil to be cleaned up, because it is too costly, or because it threatens their position or power or status or wealth, they must be challenged – I think of homeless children or adults, people with disabilities, travellers, the list goes on.

The gospel is not a political gospel – it is a gospel of compassion. But it may have to tread on political ground if it is to truly reach out to the poor and the powerless.

## 2. A church that is poor and powerless

'He has pulled down princes from their thrones and exalted the lowly. The hungry he has filled with good things, the rich sent empty away.' Why would we think that this vision does not also refer to the churches?

I believe that a church that proclaims the gospel must be a church that *is* poor and powerless. A church, rich and powerful, will be pulled down and sent empty away. A church that is poor and powerless involves a new vision of priesthood. If the criteria for priesthood emphasises the necessity to complete a third level qualification in theology and philosophy, then given the educational structure of our world and of our society, candidates for the priesthood will be drawn predominantly from middle class backgrounds. That shapes the church's expectations, aspirations, its value system, its understanding of, and attitude towards the structures of our world and our societies.

Another image I use is that of a person living in a flat on the top floor of a building. 8 o'clock in the morning comes and they pull back the curtains; the sun shines in. They look out the window into the back garden and see the freshly cut grass, the beautiful multi-coloured flowers swaying in the gentle breeze, the birds hopping on the lawn looking for worms. They think, what a beautiful day.

However, someone may be living in the basement flat of the same house. 8 o'clock in the morning comes, they pull back the curtains; nothing happens. The sun can't get in. They look out the window into the back garden and all they see is the whitewashed wall of the outside toilet; they cannot see the garden, or the grass or the flowers or the birds.

Here we have two people looking out of the same house, into the same garden, at the same time of the same day, but they have two totally different views; there is the view from the top and the view from the bottom.

If the leadership in our church comes from predominantly middle-class backgrounds, then the church will predominantly have the view from the top. To seek a church that is poor and that aspires to be poor is to seek out and welcome candidates for the priesthood from among the poor. Of course, if such candidates come into a church that is middle class, a church that aspires to a middle class quality of life, then priesthood becomes an upwardly mobile vocation choice for people who are poor, as with the Roman Catholic Church in parts of Africa today.

A church that is poor is a church that is free. Wealth and property and power tie the church into those aspirations and structures that are dominated by the comfortable and make the church less free not only to be critical, but to even realise that it ought to be critical. A church of wealth and property and power tends to be – as we have seen in Ireland – a church that accepts the status quo and is welcomed by and accepted by those whose interests lie in retaining the status quo. A church that is wealthy and powerful can never be prophetic – and our world today needs a prophetic church, it cries out for a prophetic church. Those who are poor and excluded in our society and in our world, whose dignity the church proclaims again and again from the altar, have a right to expect the church to pro-claim that dignity in the way it lives.

In Luke's gospel, the person chosen to be the mother of God was a nobody from Nazareth, a despised region of Israel; the person who first recognises Mary's honour is an elderly barren woman, Elizabeth, who would have been despised in society because of her barrenness, which was understood to be a sign of God's displeasure; and the first persons to witness to the birth of Jesus were shepherds, a despised group of people. God chose the poor and the powerless to be witnesses to, and instruments of, the salvation which Jesus came to bring. The church, which continues to witness to, and be the instrument of, God's salvation must too be poor and powerless.

*Conclusion*

The Magnificat then poses for me a two-fold challenge:

First, to enter more deeply into my experience and conviction of the unconditional love of God, given to me, not because I deserve it, or have earned it, but because I am God's creation.

Secondly, resting on this foundation and driven by gratitude, to reach out in compassion to those whose dignity as children of God is being denied or undermined, and to accept the radical, all embracing consequences of being the compassion of God, even if those consequences bring us, as they brought to Jesus, marginalisation, suffering, and, perhaps, even death.

# CHAPTER FIVE

# The Church: A People in Communion?

*Cathy Molloy*

W hy bother with the church? Why spend your energy studying/teaching theology? Don't you know people have moved on? As a woman, how can you be part of a church that seems to want you to be there but to have no real input into how things are organised? Would you accept this kind of relationship in any other context? Isn't the whole church set-up so out of line with the rest of life? I have often been asked questions like these and they are fair questions in this age of aspiring equality, when institutions in general are taking a battering, and the churches in particular are struggling to maintain credibility.

Yes, many people have 'moved on', in the sense that they no longer find institutional church structures helpful to their sense of who they are and how they relate to the ultimate concerns of human existence. For others, albeit a dwindling number, it is precisely within the church that they find a meaningful way to be in relation to those same ultimate concerns shared with all of humanity. *Who* are we? What are we *like*? What are we *for*? What should we *do*? As one of that number, I see in Jesus Christ someone who demonstrated, in the most radical way, how we might aspire to live together, and what we might hope for, in relation to the ultimate mystery we call God. As one of that number my self-understanding is moulded, to a certain extent, within the institutional church structures which continually struggle to evolve as worthy of his name. It is the relationships within these structures that are the focus of this chapter.

*What kind of involvement?*

Nowadays we have become quite used to matters of faith and of church being discussed on radio and television. People of many religions and none, men and women critical or supportive of their own faith community, their church, its teaching, leaders, laws, get quite a bit of airtime in a society where we are led to believe that most people have 'moved on'. The print media too has had a steady stream of reports, interviews and articles about church matters, all the more so, it seems, since the recent scandals have dominated all news of church from virtually every part of the world.

But what do we mean when we refer to the church? Who are we talking about? I recall, many years ago, engaging in yet another frustrating discussion about the church and what they were or were not saying or doing, being told 'but *you* are the church'. I was stopped in my tracks and stunned by the simplicity of the assertion, which has hugely affected the course of my life. The realisation that the church is *us* meant considering the whole question of belonging in a new way. Baptism is about belonging, but belonging is a two-way thing, the individual and the group are changed with each new baptising. We are baptised individually, but into the community. We belong to, we each form and are a unique expression of some aspect of, that group that is collectively called church. We are involved with each other and with the work of Jesus and those who came after him in the attempt to bring about the 'kingdom' of justice, love and peace. But what is our relationship one to the other?

In spite of forty years of the teaching church attempting to promote the notion of the church as *The People of God*, many of us still fall back on the tendency to talk about the church as though it were constituted only by the priests, bishops, cardinals and the Pope. This is understandable given the hierarchical structure of the church, and the way authority is exercised. When we hear 'the church teaches', 'the church says', 'the church should', (or should not) and so on, we tend to think immediately of faith propositions to be assented to, rules handed down to be obeyed, initiatives to be taken or discontinued. We don't necessarily think 'we teach', 'we say', 'we should'. I sense that this is changing. One of the positive things to begin to emerge from the unimagined horrors of the sexual abuse scandals is that many people have experienced themselves as church. In trying to come to terms with the painful unfolding of this reality, in our shock and anger and helplessness in the face of the suffering of the victims, and our guilt by association in the face of the handling of the fact, we have learnt something that no document from Rome, or theology book or lesson in doctrine could teach so effectively. *We are the church*. We are fundamentally linked to the victims and to the perpetrators, all are part of who we are. This is what it means to be a communion, a way of describing the church that is being developed in much recent writing of John Paul II.

*Church and Communion*
The wide use of the term communion (*koinonia*) in the New Testament shows that those who were baptized felt strongly that they had much in common.[1] The baptized are incorporated into the life, death and resurrection of Christ, become sons and daughters of God, are formed into God's people, become a new creation, share the dignity of being called children of God. 'And so what?' I often found myself thinking. So, irrespective of the details of who, or when, or where, it is clear that what we share at this fundamental level far outweighs any prior or subsequent distinctions that occur as we go through life with whatever combination of circumstances and events. So, it is a church of saints and sinners, all sharing a basic sacredness, all

1. Mc Brien, *Catholicism*, New Edition, London: Chapman, 1994, p 580.

deserving of equal respect whatever our role or position. So, the implications of this for relationships within the church are great indeed, but, in spite of the concern for justice in the world, consistent in the social teaching, they are not immediately made obvious by some of our structures. Justice, right relationship, within the church seems not to preoccupy us greatly. For so long most lay people, including religious, have passively accepted that all is handed down, that our good is best known and best decided by others. Of course we rail against things from time to time, but, as long as we can blame the hierarchy, we don't have to do anything. We are not responsible for any of it.

Karl Rahner, in *The Shape of the Church to Come*, (1967), spoke of the church of the future as a listening church, 'a church of the grassroots', a 'declericalised church', and there are small signs already of this new way of relating taking the place of the 'top down' model. The wide participation involved in the setting up of parish councils, the Women's Forum, and parish renewal groups or theology courses is indicative of a new situation. Certainly a sad fact is that these kinds of initiatives have come too little and too late for many people in the Irish church. However, for the stalwarts who remain, the signs are encouraging. The listening and sharing of responsibility regarding ways to proceed with a course for adult religious education, or a family Mass, or whatever, are, in my experience, welcomed by the vast majority of clergy and laity, and there are signs of a more inclusive church evolving. Of course not everyone is happy with the new ways. There are men and women, laity as well as clergy, people of goodwill as well as those who are fearful, who hold fast to the old, even to the extent of blocking, passively or actively, the path of the church of the future that is coming to meet us. There is fear of over-involvement of the laity. But the closing of seminaries and novitiates speaks its own language, and we all understand it. The statistics in relation to the ordained priesthood as we have known it, tell us now of what does not lie ahead. If we take seriously the church as communion, what is awaiting us is what will emerge from the ground up, from within the *whole* People of God.

The documents of Vatican II, (for example *Dogmatic Constitution on the Church, Lumen Gentium,* 6) in proclaiming the church as a sign and instrument of communion with God, and of unity among all people, point to a way of being church that is widely inclusive and in which everyone's part is significant. By definition then, there is a social dimension which is part of who we are and to ignore this is to diminish the potential of the group. There has often been the impression that the mission belongs to the hierarchy and that lay people share in this by concession. The words of John Paul give the lie to this way of seeing it when he explains what it means to say we, as church, are a communion:

> Communion speaks of a double life-giving participation: the incorporation of Christians into the life of Christ, and the communication of that life of charity to the entire body of the Faithful.[2] The reality of the church as communion is the integrating aspect, indeed the central content of the *'mystery', or rather the divine plan for the salvation of humanity.*

Baptism brings us into communion, but it is the Eucharist that sustains us in the relationship. In my understanding the eucharist is the bread of spiritual life; at one level it is literally food to keep me going. I need it for faith and for hope and for being in the love of God, which allows me to love others, and which keeps me connected when I am failing in the attempt to love. The Eucharist is not called the source and summit of our faith for no reason,

2. John Paul II, *Christifideles Laici,* (N.19), Apostolic Exhortation on the Vocation and the Mission of the Lay Faithful in the Church and in the World, Given at Rome 30 December 1988.

it is a sign and actually brings about communion among the members of the church, and with God, and is fundamental to the mission of reaching out to others which is basic to Christian living. This relationship is of the essence of Christianity. We are involved whether or not we decide to activate that involvement. For this reason the excluding of someone from full participation in Eucharistic celebration can seem counter to the meaning of communion. I have often been struck by the gospel story of the Last Supper. Jesus neither asked Judas to leave before the breaking of the bread, nor refused to share it with him. 'Take, eat, this is my body', he said, having acknowledged that one of them was his betrayer. What is this telling us about communion?

### Communion and Justice

Jesus came so that we might have life and have it to the full. All Christians share in his mission. The aims and hopes for humanity instanced in the 1948 *Universal Declaration of Human Rights*, are indicative of the minimum that is needed for human well-being. The church as communion implies that awareness of what contributes to this, or works against it, needs to be accompanied by action for justice if we are to be authentic. The 1971 Synod of Bishops, in its statement on *Justice in the World*, could not have put it more plainly:

> Action on behalf of justice and participation in the transformation of the world fully appear to us as a constitutive dimension of the preaching of the gospel (p. 6). Christian love of neighbour and justice cannot be separated. For love implies an absolute demand for justice, namely a recognition of the dignity and rights of one's neighbour. Justice attains its inner fullness only in love ... (p. 14).

The meaning of this is very clear and makes the focus

on justice essential for all in the church. We all share the responsibility for the attempt to secure the dignity and basic welfare of every human person. Whether this means participation in any of the groups working at the level of basic needs, or developing the abilities present in each human being, belonging to a peace group or supporting human rights workers, or simply consciously living our life having regard to the call to justice, is not the most important thing. What is important is that the focus on justice, within and without the church, is of the nature of being Christian. The gifts and talents of each one must be facilitated so that they truly become the gifts and talents of all, and are truly at the service of all. There can be no degrees of belonging, no hierarchy of value, no 'golden circle', no elite group set aside from the rest, in the communion described and elaborated upon by John Paul.

It is obvious that internal relationships and structures, and our relationships with other Christian churches and the world would need to reflect this if an authentic communion is being aimed at. Pope John Paul II, in the Apostolic Letter *Novo Millennio Ineuente* (Jan 2001) describes his office, the 'Petrine ministry', and that of the bishops, 'episcopal collegiality', as 'specific services to communion' (Ch. 4). In many obvious ways they are manifestly so. But bearing in mind the full implications of communion I wonder whether they can ever be truly, and not just notionally, its instruments, with so many of the communion automatically excluded from participating in them? If we really believe in the church as communion, and seek sincerely to live it more fully, then must some of the present ways of doing things be radically revised in the light of developing understanding and the desire, or indeed the demand, for authenticity?

There is a view that if we are in right relationship then surely right structures must follow. The church as communion can be a powerful motivating concept here. If we are indeed in communion with Christ and with one another, then our striving must be for the best expression of that relationship that we can achieve, and we cannot lightly continue with fundamentally unjust structures or systems. Another view puts structures first, holding that if the structures are right then right relationships will follow. This surely applies equally to gender, inter-church, and inter-faith relationships. Remy Parent in *A Church of the Baptised*, points out that priests, bishops, the Pope even, often use a vocabulary of service accompanied by behaviour patterns of power and exclusion.[3]

### Communion, Spirituality and Justice

The Apostolic Letter *Novo Millennio Ineunte,(Jan* 2001) of John Paul II, mentioned above, links the future and the theme of communion explicitly. He urges that a spirituality of communion be promoted before making practical plans, making it the 'guiding principle of education wherever individuals and Christians are formed, wherever ministers of the altar, consecrated persons, and pastoral workers are trained'.[4] He goes on to explain that a spirituality of communion means thinking of our brothers and sisters in faith as 'those who are part of me'. Communion is the basis for very different kinds of relationships between lay, cleric and religious, between men and women, relationships not of complementarity, but of interdependence and mutuality, and will be an ongoing challenge to all the members of the church.

Implications for justice issues within and outside the church are of its essence. Our brothers and sisters in faith are 'those who are part of me' whether or not they fit, or feature in, my notion of church. Where they are is where

---

3. Remy Parent, *A Church of the Baptised*, New York: Paulist Press, 1987, p 83.
4. John Paul II, *Novo Millennio Ineunte*, Apostolic Letter of John Paul II, Jan 2001, Ch. 1V Witness to Love, n. 42-44.

the church is. We are used to being encouraged to see this communion in the materially or spiritually poor and destitute, and they must be a primary concern. But they must be a concern in a new way if we are to be authentic in our attempts at communion, not as objects of pastoral concern, but as subjects who often give in many more ways than they receive. Recognising this reciprocity is one important key to our understanding of church as communion. But if we are striving to be an authentic communion we will also see it in the comfortable and careful, in the doubters and the disaffected, in the complacent and the smug. The emphasis on the distinctions within the church has dominated for so long that, while not overlooking their legitimacy, it will take real and prolonged and co-ordinated effort to truly live and work and pray together out of this fundamental principle. That said I think the principle of communion is beginning to be understood and acted upon in a way that will restore hope and give new impetus to the work for justice, and renewed energy to people working in an area that can so often be disheartening.

Communion and justice are inseparable, and there are many instances where, as church, in failing in one we fail also in the other. A more developed understanding of the church as communion would not have permitted the ongoing injustice suffered by the victims of clerical sexual abuse once the crimes were known, and indeed, the harm occasioned to all in the church would have been much lessened. If we understand the meaning of communion, our silent consent to the living conditions of those on the edge of society, travellers for example, is unacceptable, and some of the actions taken against them incompatible with Christian living. The authenticity of the church as communion is likewise diminished by the perceived, and in many cases very real, harsh treatment of people in second unions after marriage breakdown. The sidelining of so many former priests and religious, whose gifts and learning are so needed by the searching People of God, poses other questions about who we are and who we say we are. The loss of their input is incalculable. The authenticity of the church as communion can be challenged in the way that gay and lesbian Christians are often treated as objects of pastoral concern rather than subjects, active in and for the church. The refusal of further public discussion of the ordination of women also seriously challenges the sincerity of the leadership in the attempt to become the communion we profess to be.

The problems are not limited to the relationship between clergy and laity. Within the laity too are many articulate groups who loudly profess polemical views on particular issues, and whose treatment of people who are the target of their objections can give the lie to the label Christian, not to mention any notion of the church as communion.

What about the other side of the coin? Are there instances of, or experiences of the communion we profess to be which serve as examples of what we might be aiming at, the kind of church Karl Rahner described so many years ago? Isn't it fair that we should look to our church leaders to lead in this regard? There are already signs if we have eyes to see and the courage to follow. When we hear church leaders speak out or stand in solidarity, for example, with travellers in the face of tough and unpleasant opposition, or publicly reach out to those on the edge because of their marital situation, we are shown what the church as communion implies. When women and men, lay, priests and religious, work together for justice, solidarity, education, peacemaking, when they worship together, in shared acknowledgement of who God is and what God has done for us, communion can be experienced as something real. Then such concepts, and indeed realities, as hierarchy, authority, power, and control, cease to occupy the positions of exaggerated importance that are too fre-

quently afforded them, and instead are reduced to the
dimensions proper to them. Here we can begin to see a
church whose institutional aspects are genuinely at the service of all the People of God. But how can we bring these
isolated experiences of communion more to the centre of
what it is to be the church?

*Further Justice Issues: Education and Solidarity*
Justice issues are to the fore in terms of access to the
knowledge as well as the experience of what it is to be
church. One challenge for today is at the fundamental
level of education. Have people meaningful access to the
teaching and traditions of their church? If the teaching of
the church is explained in too narrow a set of terms then
many are excluded from an understanding of faith which
should be theirs. If the gap between the language and concepts of the culture and the terms in which faith issues are
couched is too wide, as it seems to be for many today, then
surely the onus is on the theologians, the priests and the
teachers, not only to find ways to articulate teaching that is
faithful and accessible at once, but also to help people to
articulate their religious longings, their desires in respect
of God?

There is new emphasis on education or formation as it
is called in *Christifideles Laici*, the 1988 Apostolic Exhortation
of John Paul II on the laity. This 'is not the privilege of a
few but the right and the duty of all' (n 63).The implications of this are only beginning to emerge. We educate,
form, one another. There is need for lay men and women
to be involved, alongside clergy and religious, in the ongoing work of the church that theology is. The justice issues
are hovering at different levels. Which men and women?
Only those who have money enough for fees for colleges
of theology and philosophy? Which priests and religious?
Only those who have a proven record regarding stances in

the face of particular moral positions? The People of God, in faith, seeking understanding, may come up with some very different and enriching understandings than is the case when only particular clerical people of God are the recognised seekers. Examples would be the whole area of Liberation Theology – people reflecting on faith from their own situation of injustice and oppression, and the contribution of women theologians in all areas of theology.

*Solidarity as the way forward*
The ongoing attempt at 'ordering creation to the authentic well-being of humanity' is a specific task for Christians, women and men, lay, cleric, and religious. Solidarity with one another and with all humanity is a necessary means and method for achieving this. Church teaching describes it as 'a firm and persevering determination to commit oneself to the *common good ... because ... we are all really responsible for all'* (*Christifideles Laici*, n 42). In this understanding no one is left out. The suffering and death of innocent people, near and far, is our concern. The suffering and death of guilty people, near and far, is equally a concern in the Christian perspective. Communion is a gift to be lived in the light of the ever-present challenge to become who we are. Solidarity with those who are out of the frame for whatever reason, must be central to our striving. Action for justice to enable all people to claim and enjoy their rightful participation in the beauty and goods of our world, must be at the heart of our faith and love, but in a way that acknowledges the space between what we may do and who God is, in whom we ultimately hope.

# CHAPTER SIX

# The Eucharist, reconciliation and politics

*Brian Lennon SJ*

Our theme in this book is the link between theology and spirituality on the one hand and social justice issues on the other. I live and work in Northern Ireland where justice is a much contested term: Republicans claimed they were fighting for it; Unionists say they are deprived of it under the 1998 Good Friday Agreement. In this article I will look at the links between the Eucharist and reconciliation, a concept which is broader than justice and includes it. As will become clear, however, 'reconciliation' as a concept is also fraught with difficulties.

Christian reconciliation includes forgiving, repenting, justice and truth. These were not dealt with in the Good Friday Agreement and in their absence reconciliation talks tend to place an unbalanced burden on victims/survivors. Of course reconciliation is used by many in ways that are not connected with all the elements of Christian reconciliation. My problem with these approaches is that logically the term 'reconciliation' suggests some time in the past when parties were not divided and this is often not the case. Secondly, behind the terms, but often unstated, lie one or more of the ideas of forgiving, repenting, justice and truth.

To unpack the discussion first I will look briefly at the politics of our situation. Then I will outline two theological themes arising from the Eucharist. One is that the Eucharist is essentially a community event: in it the community is brought by Christ into the presence of God. Secondly, the God into whose presence Christ brings us is a community of Three Persons. Finally, given that taking part in the Eucharist involves a call and a commitment to community, I will look at some positive and negative uses in Northern Ireland politics of the concept of reconciliation and ask how Christians might respond to this call to community.

## 1. Political Realities

The politics of Northern Ireland were transformed by the Good Friday Agreement of 10 April 1998. The London and Dublin governments plus ten of the parties, including those connected with Republican and Loyalist paramilitaries, accepted it.

The Agreement is full of language about reconciliation. For example in the 'Declaration of Support' it says the best way to honour victims/survivors of the conflict is to: 'firmly dedicate ourselves to the achievement of reconciliation, tolerance and mutual trust' (para 2).

The Agreement also says: 'we will endeavour to strive in every practical way towards reconciliation and rapprochement within the framework of democratic and agreed arrangements' (para 5).

Similar language can be found throughout earlier documents in the peace process such as the Anglo-Irish Agreement of 1985 and the Downing Street Declaration of 1993. Yet by the Autumn of 2002, four and a half years after the signing of the Agreement, divisions between Unionists and Nationalists remained deep, the institutions set up under the Agreement had been suspended for the *fourth* time, and Unionists and Republicans were locked into mutual recriminations. Both sides had made costly compromises in accepting the Agreement, yet few in either group had much understanding of the pain the other side had suffered.

*Unionist compromises and perceptions*
Under the Agreement Unionists accepted power-sharing,

not only with the SDLP, but also with their greatest enemies, Sinn Féin. They accepted North-South structures and had to tolerate the early release of prisoners. As the process developed, however, their opposition to the Agreement increased. They argued that Republicans had not committed themselves to non-violence because they failed to decommission their weapons and because the IRA continued to exist. Under great pressure, Republicans eventually decommissioned weapons on several occasions, but four years after the signing of the Agreement the IRA was still active. Allegedly it imported weapons, murdered alleged drug-dealers, carried out punishment beatings and shootings in local estates. It also refused to recognise the new Police Service. It was alleged they were involved in major robberies, in a break-in at the Castlereagh holding centre which captured important intelligence material, and in spying on the British and Irish governments and other parties, and continuing to gather intelligence on security force personnel. Three Sinn Féin members were also caught in Columbia allegedly giving explosives training to FARC guerrillas. In these circumstances a majority of Unionists seems to have concluded that they cannot share government with Sinn Féin until the IRA is disbanded.

*Republican compromises and perceptions*
In the past Republicans defined the problem as the presence of the British in Ireland. The answer was to remove them. As they saw it, this could only be done through violence. Yet, slowly but surely throughout the mid- to late-1980s and 1990s they changed. Under the 1998 Agreement they moved from opposing a Northern Ireland Assembly to being strong supporters of it, they took two ministries in the government appointed by the Assembly (a government which derives its powers through the Assembly from the British parliament in Westminster), they accepted the deletion of the South's constitutional claim over

Northern Ireland, and North-South structures which had fewer powers than they had sought. They took offices at the Westminster parliament although they refused to take their seats. They said they would never decommission weapons but then destroyed some weapons on three occasions before the end of 2001. These changes were achieved without a major split among Republicans. Given these compromises republicans see the fact that the Executive has been terminated four times as a sign of bad faith on the part of both the British government and Unionists, and they see the emphasis on Republicans' violence as unwarranted, given the greater level of Loyalist violence. The Derry based Pat Finucane Centre listed over 60 sectarian attacks involving Loyalists, including pipe bombs, stabbings and the murder of 19 year old Gerard Lawler in July 2002.

*The Community Response*
The picture at a community level is very mixed. There are many peace groups working effectively in different situations and, I believe, making a real impact. Yet many believe sectarianism has deepened since the 1998 Agreement. A symptom of this was the interface street violence in North Belfast. This continuing community-level conflict highlights the limits of the Agreement. In many ways it was a fudged document which allowed politicians to support it while maintaining opposed positions. The continuing disagreements between politicians, Unionist fears of a united Ireland, and continuing power struggles between paramilitaries, all fuel the community conflict. The Agreement did not focus sufficiently on the community response and this remains a continuing threat to the survival of the institutions. Cut backs in European funding in 2002 added to these problems.

My own main work is with a group called Community

Dialogue.[1] We organise programmes within and between groups of Unionists, Loyalists, Nationalists, Republicans and others. These are aimed at increasing the level of understanding, principally by focusing on what individuals want most deeply in the area of politics, and also by encouraging people to outline the experiences which have led them to hold these positions. We also produce leaflets outlining different views. After centuries of conflict people on the ground will need long, slow hard dialogue before they can make peace.

In summary, then, the 1998 Agreement had a vision of reconciliation, but the conflict in Northern Ireland continued to fester. The Agreement formally recognised the right of each group to a veto. This means that Unionists will not be able to exercise power in a devolved government without Sinn Féin and vice versa. Both sides at different times are in a degree of denial about this. Despite this, the picture four years after the signing of the Agreement was vastly better than it had been during the Troubles.

## 2. SOME THEOLOGICAL NOTES ON THE EUCHARIST[2]

### a: The communal nature of the Eucharist

In turning to some eucharistic themes there will be quite a shift in tone between this and the previous section.

### (i) The Eucharist makes us present to a past event

In the New Testament both Paul and Luke report Jesus at the end of the Last Supper as saying 'Do this in remembrance of me.' The Jewish notion of memory at the time was quite different from ours. We remember past events simply as past. They may still affect us, but they are over.

1. Information on the group is available from: Community Dialogue, 373 Springfield Road, Belfast BT12 7DG, email: admin@commdial.org. Publications of the group are available at: www.commdial.org.
2. This section has been adapted from my article 'Who should come to the Eucharist?', *The Furrow*, Volume 52, Number 10, October 2001, pp 532-538.

For Jews, when they came together to celebrate a religious event such as the Passover, they were of course remembering events in their past history. In the case of the Passover it was the central event which had made them into a people: the freeing of the Jewish people from slavery in Egypt. But they were doing more than this. They did not see the Passover as simply past. Rather in the Passover God acted to free not only their ancestors but the Jewish people as a whole, past and present. They were incapable of thinking of themselves in a way parallel to modern individualism. For them the community was a far more dominant notion than that of the individual. So when they celebrated the Passover they saw God saving them just as he had saved their ancestors, because they and their ancestors were one people. In this way therefore they were caught up into – made present to – the original Passover event.

By putting the words 'Do this in memory of me' into the mouth of Jesus at the Last Supper both Paul and Luke are trying to communicate something of the same notion. The early Christians believed, when they celebrated the Lord's Supper, that they too were caught up in, made present to, the original Last Supper. Sacramentally, they were gathered together with the disciples around the table. Together with Christ they were drawn into the journey from the supper, to the garden, the trial, the way of the cross, into the experience of Christ who subjected himself to bloody impotence, to the finality of the death, and then, amazingly, they join Christ sacramentally in the miracle of the resurrection.

(ii) Who is included?
Christ died so that everyone might be saved. The Jews who first followed Christ were slow to realise this. It was St Paul who broke through the barrier of seeing God's community confined to the Jewish people, and he did this at the cost of a deep struggle with the Jerusalem-based

church. Indeed there is evidence in the gospel that Jesus himself had to learn that God's plan was for the Gentiles as well as the Jews: the Canaanite woman (Mt 15), and the Centurion whose servant he cured (Mt 8:5) both surprised him with their faith and led him to say that many non-Jews will sit down in heaven. Sinners were also part of the community. He sat at table – and this meant entering into a relationship – with the prostitutes and tax collectors (without any prior repentance on their part). He preached forgiveness for enemies, but he also made social relationships a pre-condition for worship: 'So if you are about to offer your gift to God at the altar and there remember that your brother or sister has something against you, leave your gift there in front of the altar, go at once and make peace with your brother or sister, and then come back to offer your gift' (Mt 5:23).

A Jesuit guru, Tony de Mello, used to remark that God is at least as good as the best of us. If the vast majority of people – and we are made in the image of God – would be unable to let go of their children no matter what they did, can we imagine God being able to do so? The Cross is about God in Christ drawing the whole world into community with himself, not through the power of force, but through the apparent powerlessness of truth, forgiveness and love.

In the Eucharist, then, we are called to build a human community on earth, to make peace with our enemies, and to include sinners in our community (in part because we are sinners ourselves), and we cannot relate to the God revealed by Jesus Christ unless we do this.

*b: The nature of God*
This focus on community is strengthened when we look at the nature of God. The central truth about the Christian God is that God is three Persons in one divine essence. In practice the Trinity is one of the most neglected of

Christian teachings. This seems a pity, particularly when considering an issue like reconciliation, because one consequence of the doctrine of the Trinity is that the essence of God is to be found in community, and reconciliation, at its most obvious level, seems to be about re-establishing community.

There are historical reasons why the Trinity tends to have such limited appeal to Christians. One is that traditionally the emphasis was first on proving the existence of God from natural philosophy. In this the focus was on God as one, unchanging, and therefore essentially relating to God. At the same time the Scriptures, as distinct from natural philosophy, are very strong on the unique roles of the Father, the Son and the Spirit. In the Gospels Christ speaks constantly of his love for the Father, of the Father for him, and – especially in John's Gospel – of their oneness.

This point is not merely academic. It impacts on our human assumptions about the centrality of relationships among people. Are these mere incidentals to our lives as we pass in and out of family, marriage and political relationships? Or are they part of something much greater: glimpses of our call to be humans created in the image of Three Persons who are in love with each other and who draw us into their love?

## c. The Eucharist and Community

There is an intrinsic link between the individual, the community, the Eucharist and the community of Three Persons in God. One cannot relate to God without relating to the community. (This echoes the theme of the Covenant Community in the Old Testament). Taking part in the Eucharist and pretending or thinking that one is actually doing this in any effective way without also being open to and committed to relating to the community, makes no sense. To do so would be like saying we want to relate to God on our own, and go to the Eucharist in the hope of such a privatised or exclusive celebration. But at the Eucharist we are caught up into Christ's life, death and resurrection and that life, death and resurrection was about creating a community of respect. That community includes not only those who take part in the Eucharist, but all those God in Christ wants to be part of it, namely every human being. This community came from God as part of creation, it is made in the image of God who is Three, it is called to go back to the community of the Three, and only in God will we ultimately find what we are looking for, because it is for God that we have been made.

The Eucharist, then, and the Christian life, is inherently social and inclusive. Because of Christ's teaching and life we are called to repent of our sins against others, to forgive, to seek justice for all, to open ourselves to truth. We are called to do this both as individuals and as Christian groups. And without seeking to do this we can have no part with Christ, although God will never cease to find new ways to attempt to draw us into community.

## 3. THE CHRISTIAN VISION AND POLITICS

### Reconciliation

Many argue that an appropriate interface between the Christian vision of community and politics is reconciliation. Is it? How does Christian reconciliation relate to politics? What connects the Christian vision of Christ bringing the whole world into the community of the Trinity, the vision expressed in a document like the Good Friday Agreement, and the reality of life on the ground in Northern Ireland as different groups struggle with each other?

### The Good Friday Agreement and Reconciliation

As we saw above, the opening passages of the Agreement stress the commitment of the participants to reconciliation. It also emphasises tolerance, mutual trust, the protection

of human rights, partnership, equality, respect, rapprochement, a spirit of concord, the use of exclusively democratic
means, and their opposition to the use of, or threat of, force
for political ends. Concretely these ideals are applied
through the principle of consent – that there will be no
change in the constitutional status of Northern Ireland
without the consent of the majority, both North and South
– and the new institutions set up under the Agreement.
The hope is that these will create a better context for the
future. What the Agreement does not do is deal with the
past. There is no requirement for justice, truth, repentance
or forgiveness. I am not arguing there should have been,
but if reconciliation includes these, then the Agreement,
while it talks about reconciliation, does not *deal* with it, at
least in terms of dealing with the past. If this is true, then it
does not help matters for the Agreement to outline a vision
of reconciliation because, as I will argue below, the end
result is that an unfair burden is laid on victims/survivors
and perpetrators get off scot free. If the Agreement is
thinking of some other concept of reconciliation, what is it?

The method the Agreement uses to deal with the past is
amnesia. Prisoners are released early. Technically they are
out on licence and so can be recalled to finish their sen-
tence if convicted of other offences. There is no commitment to enquiries into human rights abuses by either the
security forces or paramilitaries. By contrast, in South
Africa amnesty was linked to a requirement to tell the
truth.

Given the context of the Agreement, is Christian reconciliation a useful concept for us in Northern Ireland?

*1: Arguments against the usefulness of Reconciliation*
(i) The many meanings of reconciliation
One problem with the use of the term reconciliation is the
varieties of meanings attributed to it.
• Some discussions include references to forgiving, re-

pentance, justice or truth. Others use reconciliation and forgiveness interchangeably. Some discussions use none of these concepts and simply look at ways to reduce violence.

- Usage also varies greatly depending on whether one is discussing religious, political/legal, socio-economic, or social psychological issues.

The vast variety of meanings intended by the term reduce its value as a concept because in every instance we need to ask people what they are talking about. Christian reconciliation is certainly tied in with forgiving, repenting, justice and truth. Are these concepts helpful?

(ii) Forgiving and repenting

In Northern Ireland reconciliation is often used interchangeably with forgiveness, sometimes in potentially destructive ways. It can refer to forgiving offered by the victim, or to a plea for forgiveness by the perpetrator. In my experience most reconciliation statements in Northern Ireland emphasise the former. Consider the following statements: 'Northern Ireland needs forgiveness above all else', and 'We all need to forgive' (a statement often made by non-victims/survivors!). How will these be received by those involved? Victims/survivors often hear such statements as meaning there is something wrong with them if they fail to forgive. Perpetrators can hear them as meaning they don't have to do anything until forgiveness is offered to them. If they take the view, as many paramilitaries and individual abusers of human rights in the security forces do, that their violence was justified, then it's not their problem at all.

People often talk of forgiving as an ability to 'move on', to come to a stage where one's life is not dominated by the injustice. To get to that stage is to do something extraordinary. Entirely innocent people who suffer an appalling injustice are faced with the task of moving on or else being stuck in the depths of bitterness.

For the Christian, however, forgiving means something more: not only moving beyond any notion of revenge, but also being open in principle to a new relationship with the perpetrator. This is clear both from God's acceptance of us 'while we were still sinners' (Roms 5:6), and the constant reaching out by Christ to sinners: e.g. his table fellowship with tax collectors was certainly with some people who had not repented.

It is critically important, especially for those of us who are not victims/survivors, not to add to the burdens of victims/survivors, particularly by a misplaced and/or mistimed reference to Christ's call and example of offering forgiveness. We need to put the ideal of forgiving before victims/survivors. But we do a great injustice if, in so doing, we help them to feel guilty or a failure because they have not been able to scale the heights of forgiving. Getting the right balance in this is not easy: if we adopt the position that victims/survivors should not be challenged we can in some way dehumanise them. We subtly reinforce the view that their lives must forever be dominated totally by the injustice they have faced. Doing this would help to keep them in the victim box and block them from becoming survivors. But to focus on the task of forgiving, without at least as much focus on repentance, truth and justice, or to assume that everyone is capable of the same degree of forgiving, would be equally wrong.

We also need to stress the detailed steps needed to move towards forgiveness. If we are going to climb Mount Everest we plan a series of camps on the way up. Telling people they have not reached the summit when they are moving from the first to the second camp does not help. Encouraging and respecting a victim who gets through one more day without killing a perpetrator may be far more appropriate than a lecture on the infinite love of God.

Why do so many in a conflict situation – especially Christians – put so much stress on the ideal of forgiving, while failing to put as much emphasis on other virtues, for example, financial probity or chastity, especially as victims/survivors are likely to be among the most vulnerable people in the world? This is not a plea to minimise the importance of forgiving: it is surely at the centre of the Christian's call. It is rather a call for balance. By all means let us stress forgiving, but only in a context where we put as much stress on the need for repenting, justice and truth, as well as other virtues.

Finally we need to ask what is our own role in any particular situation. While admitting overlaps, am I a victim, a perpetrator or neither? In each case we have different tasks. Perpetrators need to repent, victims/survivors need to start the long journey towards forgiving. Those of us who are neither victims/survivors nor perpetrators in a particular incident need to stress justice rather than the need to forgive. Justice is something we may be able to do something about, whereas forgiving or repenting is not, since we are neither victims/survivors nor perpetrators. If we want to preach to others we should start with perpetrators, not victims/survivors, and focus on apology, restitution, punishment and restorative justice. Statements like 'We must all forgive', when issued by non-victims/survivors, can be exercises in laying burdens on others which we do not have to carry ourselves. So the context from which we speak is hugely important.

We need more discussion about different aspects of forgiving and to avoid simplifying it. As one person at a conference said: 'When the Agreement came they told us we had to forgive. Now we realise we face layer upon layer of complexity'.

(iii) Justice and Truth
Both justice and truth are desperately needed by victims/survivors and they are entitled to them. The reality is,

however, that they will not get them under the Good
Friday Agreement.

As we saw above, unlike South Africa, early release in
Northern Ireland was not linked to any requirement to tell
the truth. Yet there has been pressure for enquiries into
past human rights abuses. This is mainly coming from the
Republican and Nationalist side but only into incidents in
which the security forces were allegedly at fault. The government, for reasons of political expediency, has conceded
several of these. (The Bloody Sunday enquiry is in a different category: It was needed to undo the untruths in the last
official enquiry by Widgery.) This means there is a lack of
balance in the situation – some security force abuses will
be investigated officially, but no paramilitary ones. In response, Unionist groups are now looking for enquiries.
One reaction is to argue that state abuses are worse and so
should be investigated. Further, paramilitary abuses were
investigated in the courts, security force abuses were not,
at least not in an acceptable process. But the Good Friday
Agreement dealt with this issue by deciding to say nothing about investigating the past, so why now should we be
investigating the past at all, unless we want to renegotiate
the Agreement? In the absence of enquiries there are other
options for dealing with the past, such as story telling, an
annual remembrance day, a living museum and others
outlined in the work of the *Healing Through Remembering
Project* in Northern Ireland.[3]

The Agreement, despite the sentiments in its opening
'Declaration of Support' is not about Christian reconciliation. Nor should it have been. It was a pragmatic attempt
to create a series of political structures in which enemies
could work together without killing each other.

*(2) Positive elements in Christian Reconciliation in Politics?*
The discussion so far has been fairly critical of reconcilia-

3. Unit 4, River's Edge, 15 Ravenhill Road, Belfast BT6 8DN, June 2002.

tion language in politics. What positive elements are there in it?

Individual Christians are obviously called to work for an end to destructive conflict in politics and society and their example can encourage others. Yet here again we need to be cautious because others, who have apparently been unable to make much progress in forgiveness, can feel discouraged and guilty as they look at the example of prominent people who have managed to move. The answer to this is for each person to focus on what he or she can do. God asks no more than this.

Individual leaders can play an important role and make a wider impact on society. An obvious example is Nelson Mandela. Think of the difference there would have been in the South African situation had he not forgiven (and the word is totally appropriate in his case) the National Party leaders for his 27 years in prison.

But the Christian story is at least as much about groups as it is about individuals. It's about God forgiving the people, about the people repenting and being called to 'do justice, to love mercy and to walk humbly with your God' (Mic 6:8). Does reconciliation have a role with groups as well?

The answer is certainly 'Yes' for Christian groups such as churches. It is the task of the church to witness to God's community in the world. Its continuing failure to do so is part of the human condition but none the less scandalous. The church is called in its practice – much more than its preaching – to be a living witness to God's reconciliation with us and our call to be reconciled with each other in order to relate to the God who is community.

Reconciliation is clearly a useful concept in discussions of interpersonal conflict, but as we move from inter-personal, to inter-group, to intra-State, to inter-State conflict it becomes more problematic. We can see this by focusing on repentance. At the political level two issues arise in relation to it. One is responsibility, which can mean different things depending on the context. For example, Nazis were responsible for murdering millions of Jews. In that sense they are guilty. Their children are not guilty. However, it is arguable that their children, precisely because of the sins of their fathers, have a responsibility to Jewish people. A second issue is representation. The German state took on board the guilt of the Nazis and made some restitution to Israel, which in turn was accepting a role as representing the Jewish victims/survivors. An individual German who was entirely innocent of any crime against Jews could argue that his taxes should not have been used to make compensation. But his argument fails because it is based on individualism and overlooks the fact that he is part of a community.

Nonetheless, the notions of responsibility and representation are difficult to apply. Because of this, forgiving and repenting at an intra- or inter-State level are in turn problematic. An individual who does wrong needs to repent: that involves admitting the wrong, taking responsibility, seeking to make restitution, being open to receiving just punishment. What does it mean for a state to repent? Is it appropriate to call on the British government to apologise for the Famine? On the one hand the people of England today are not responsible for the sins of their ancestors. On the other there is a connection between the British people of today and their 19th century forbears. To take a different example: reconciliation in Northern Ireland, if it is to include forgiving and repenting, would in my view need an apology by ex-paramilitaries for their campaign of violence and by individuals or branches of the security forces for human rights abuses. But most people in these categories I meet defend their past violence and seem most unlikely to change their view on this. If we say our aim is reconciliation – including repentance – it is likely to make work aimed at ending conflict more rather than less difficult. Both these examples highlight the point that reconciliation works better with individuals, in this case individual English and Irish people, than it will with the UK as a country or with a particular paramilitary organisation such as the IRA.

In the end the key question in any particular case may not be: is forgiveness or apology by a group or institution logically appropriate, but rather will either actually move the problem forward positively or not? Actions always speak louder than words: some years ago a former RUC officer told me he did not want an apology for the bomb that had crippled him twenty years previously and left him in continuous pain, but he did want an end to punishment shootings by paramilitaries. Why? Because then there would be more hospital beds free to deal with pain relief.

Some people use the term reconciliation without any intention to refer to forgiving, repentance, justice or truth. What then are they talking about? Is it a return to some previously idyllic situation which certainly did not exist in Northern Ireland? Or is it a move forward into the future without dealing with the past? This may be an appropriate aim but it is difficult to see what reconciliation can mean in this context. Further, in practice, people often refer to symbolic actions which are aimed at communicating some aspect of forgiving, repentance, justice or truth, and we end up back with something akin to the Christian notion of reconciliation.

Finally, work aimed at reducing violent conflict is often not about relationship building at all but about attempting to end a negative relationship. In these instances reconciliation seems an inappropriate term. It would, for example, be a great achievement if both sides involved in an interface riot could be persuaded to forget about each other, go their separate ways, and take up swimming! Some argue that the separate existence implied in this comment is

either not possible in Northern Ireland, or that if people remain separated the conflict will continue. In this view the
only way forward is to build positive relationships. I remain agnostic on this. It is of course obviously preferable
to build positive relationships, but separation as a strategy
should not be dismissed in all situations.

*Conclusion*

How then should Christians attempt to apply their vision
to politics, especially in the context of Northern Ireland?
The answer, as I have argued, will be easier at the level of
individuals than of groups.

As individuals all Christians are called to be reconciled
with their enemies, to do all in their power to forgive, to
repent, to work for justice and truth in their personal relationships and society. As individuals we can make an
impact both by the way we deal with our own internal
church divisions and by our work for peace in society.
Church leaders can help by showing an appreciation of the
spirituality and worship of other churches. As part of this
we need continuing progress to bring the laws of the
Catholic Church into harmony both with the changes
Vatican II, especially its recognition that sharing in sacra-
ments is a means of grace (*Decree on Ecumenism*, para 8),
and with developments in shared understanding between
churches since then. Political leaders can make an impact
by showing a public understanding of the pain of their
opponents.

In Northern Ireland, because the Agreement does not
deal with justice or truth-telling, there is a danger that an
unfair burden falls on victims/survivors. Because of this,
on balance I now believe that talk of reconciliation at the
level of politics in Northern Ireland is unhelpful. An acceptance of this would help us focus on areas which are
part of, and related to, both forgiving and repenting, but

which do not go as far as them. Among these is the issue of resentment.

Christians need to let go of resentment and challenge others to do the same, particularly if, as is often the case, those most bitter are the people who seem to have suffered least. Part of this can involve asking groups to specify what they are angry about and then asking what they want the perpetrators to do. For example, a discussion with Nationalists angry at past abuses by the British government, or Unionists angry at the IRA, can lead to an analysis of actual and perceived wrongs, *and a discussion of* restitution, apology, and the limits of justice. Showing that situations are not simple, giving people time to vent their anger, and then asking them what they want their enemies to do, can help to diffuse resentment to an extent.

We need to get to a stage where we are no longer dominated by the past, where paramilitary groups no longer exist (however difficult this may appear). Republicans need to accept the new police force, Unionists to commit themselves to working with Republicans, and we need stable devolved institutions, where there is a strong opposition and a real opportunity for voters to change the government. We need to develop a culture of non-violence and respect for difference. And we need to start contributing to the bigger world picture and play a role in an evolving Europe.

We can do all this without asking anyone to forgive, or repent, and without pretending we are moving towards justice, although elements of all three may be involved, and clearly the more that individuals make progress in all three the better for everyone.

There are a number of other concrete steps which could help us move forward. At the time of writing the Executive has been suspended. I believe it will be resurrected simply because this is in the interests of so many groups. Nonetheless there are changes which would be beneficial in the medium to long-term future. One is to change the rules of the Assembly so that it would be easier to change the government. Under current rules four parties at least are likely to end up holding ministries.

A second need is to move away from the sectarian head count which is central to the Assembly. This was necessary to deal with a divided society, but we should find ways of moving out of this within 10-15 years of the Agreement's life. This will be difficult because any move will threaten current interests.

A third suggestion is that all the parties in Northern Ireland develop a new allegiance to Northern Ireland, irrespective of its constitutional context. Whether Northern Ireland becomes part of a United Ireland – which seems very unlikely – or remains part of the UK, there will still be a need for devolved government. It is inconceivable that, having experienced the benefits of devolution, Northern Irish politicians would give these up for ever. Further, there will always need to be safeguards for minorities. Given these realities, both Unionists and Republicans, as well as others, could commit themselves to Northern Ireland while retaining their current aspirations to move towards a United Ireland or remain in the UK. If such an allegiance were expressed in flags, emblems, and anthems it would add a useful ideological basis, currently missing, because while the Agreement stresses respect for difference it does not set out an ideological base for any underlying unity.

Of course Christians will validly disagree among themselves about what concrete political steps we should support and there are arguments against a common allegiance to Northern Ireland on the grounds that it may be unachievable and we may be able to survive without it. Because of this we need continually to examine our criteria. Among those which seem important are:

- Is the proposal likely to lead to a reduction of violence?
- Will it help people's personal safety?
- Will it help or hinder sectarianism?

- Will it challenge people to deal with the past?
- Will it help them give space to other identities and traditions?

The Christian vision of community can also be helped in politics by: nuancing public positions so that more of the truth comes out; exposing the humbug that sometimes passes for reconciliation; challenging people about the consequences of their positions (Unionists on the naïve idea that they can renegotiate the Agreement to exclude Sinn Féin, Republicans on the negative consequences of their continued involvement in paramilitarism); showing people the disasters that lie ahead if we fail; offering people the vision of giving hope to the world by a successful handling of our problem of two minorities (Nationalists in the context of Northern Ireland, Unionists in the context of the whole island); increasing understanding through dialogue; and working for a democratic society.

We can replace talk of 'reconciliation' with language such as: 'dealing with the past', 'moving beyond violent conflict', 'building a future in which different groups will be secure', 'building a democratic society', which puts pressure on paramilitaries and governments to act according to international norms. We can talk of 'healing' which has some advantages over 'reconciliation': it does not presuppose the relational aspects of reconciliation and it has no necessary connotations of forgiving, repenting, justice and truth. This means that we can deal with these more directly when and as we need to do so.

Finally, we need as well to lift our eyes and hearts to the promise of God, a promise made to us again and again in all the events and personal encounters in our lives. The Eucharist is a particular example of this: by being caught up into the presence of the Three Persons who are in love with each other and with us, we are invited to enter into community in the here and now with those with whom we will share eternal life: all of us on the planet, particularly our enemies. A Christian who takes part in the Eucharist does not have the option of standing aside from peace work when the surrounding context is one of destructive conflict, unless circumstances prevent this. The way we respond, as we have seen, is complex and our responses may look small, but they are part of a bigger picture which we cannot see. There will always be a gap between the Christian vision and what we can achieve in politics. We need a language that can both keep the Christian vision before us and at the same time specify more accurately the compromises we must make in politics.

Christopher Reeves, whose spinal chord was severed in an accident in 1995, said: 'I find it's best to think, well, what can I do today? Is there something I can accomplish, a phone call I can make, a letter I can write, a person I can talk to, that will move things forward? We have to learn to live a new life that would not have seemed possible. But that's not something you need to be Superman to accomplish.'[4]

4. *Irish Times*, 21 Sep 02.

# CHAPTER SEVEN

# Women and Social Spirituality
## Towards a Third Generation Perspective

*Bernadette Flanagan PBVM*

On December 21, 2002 the result of the *Sunday Tribune* search for the greatest Irish person was announced. Nano Nagle came in first, one of only thirteen women who made the list of notable people. In doing so she came in ahead of such more widely known persons such as Michael Collins (2nd), John Hume (5th) and Oscar Wilde (15th). Many features of her life as an activist on behalf of the poor are worthy of reflection in the task of constructing a contemporary spirituality of social concern. What I believe is most important about her contribution in this field however is not those features, notable though they are, which might be repeated today. I have in mind here key features of her work like her recognition of the power of working with children in changing the life of a nation and the consequent special call to listen to voice of children in the work for justice. The challenge instead, which the life of a radical social reformer like Nano Nagle puts before us, is how to acquire her type of imagination rather than how to replicate her actions today.

## First Generation Disturbances

Nano Nagle had to struggle with how give expression to her social concern. Her society offered her a model, which, at first, she acted on intuitively. In Ireland there had been a long tradition of white martyrdom, of leaving home and family in response to the call of the gospel to leave everyone and everything. Nano had heard the call of the gospel in the misery of the tenants she met on the family farm in Cork. In response she followed the familiar path and went to a convent in continental Europe. In this way she gave symbolic expression to the total giving of herself to prayer for relief from misery for her people.

There she could hope to follow the austere way of life characteristic of Irish monasticism. Her spiritual ancestors imposed severe penances on themselves. A very unique form of penance developed in the monastic way of life. The evangelisation of Ireland had taken place without bloodshed whereas many early Christians in the empire had had to shed their blood for their faith. The monks, therefore, in an effort to suffer for Christ, undertook to leave their native country forever. This was known as 'white martyrdom'. They travelled as far north as Iceland and Greenland and east to Jerusalem and Kiev.

However, Nano's choice did not bring her the spiritual consolation it offered to her ancestors. Turmoil erupted in her inner self. Her sleep was disturbed with voices and images of those she had left behind in Ireland in order that she could serve them with undivided attention in intercession. She had the courage to give voice to this disturbance and to act on the advice that she was offered. It is easy to underestimate the challenges that this decision posed. She was the inheritor of a tradition of social concern that had given emphasis to Jesus withdrawing to lonely places in order to struggle with the social manifestation of evil. In leaving the convent in Flanders the fusion she aimed to achieve of two key strands in her life – a lively attentiveness to the divine and a deep compassion for the poor – had been ripped asunder. What would help her weave them back together again?

The effort to weave them back together was her lifetime's task. It was a challenge that led her up many cul-de-sacs. At first she did not entertain the task of reuniting the two strands in her own life. She left it to others, such as the

Ursulines, a continental religious institute that she believed could carry her vision forward. Again, however, she faced the pain of discovering that the structures of Ursuline spirituality, particularly an enclosed form of life, meant that the good news was not walking the streets. Such was her conviction of the necessity for an evolutionary leap in the form of a faith-based expression of social concern that in her fifties she eventually decided to go about giving it a form in her own life.

Then began an endless process of consultation and research to find precedents for the vision she was intuiting. Again she looked to the European continent where she found precedents that gave expression to her own inspiration, such as the way of life of the Infant Jesus Sisters founded by Fr Nicholas Barré in 1677.

One event perhaps symbolises most clearly the contours of Nano Nagle's vision for a spirituality of social concern. On Christmas Eve 1775 she moved from the comfortable suburbs of Cork, where she had for so long resided, to an inner-city cottage. In the spirit of the festive season being celebrated when she moved, she took on to unite her life with that of Love embodied in lowly conditions. It would be by immersion in the environment of those who were poor that she would be true to her God. The fact that she died before finding a definitive text that captured her vision may leave a happy space for subsequent developments. It is to this question that I now turn.

*Second Generation Philanthropy and Social Spirituality*
A spirituality of high immersion in social struggles became the characteristic spirituality of several women who lived at the time of or subsequent to Nano Nagle. In Dublin Teresa Mulally, a milliner whose fortunes were changed by a lottery win and in collaboration with James Mulcaile, a local priest who had been a Jesuit before the suppression of the Society, laboured in George's Hill and

surrounding districts for liberation from the bondage imposed by illiteracy and poverty by establishing schools.
The innovative, religiously-motivated responses of other
women like Catherine McAuley, Mary Aikenhead, Margaret
Aylward, Frances Ball and Margaret Anne Cusack found
outward expression in home visitation, health-care services, orphanages, refuges and many other initiatives. The
socio-religious enterprises of most of these women eventually became institutionalised in convents, though Catherine
McAuley left records of the fact that it was never her intention to found a congregation but simply to do as the gospel
required. The blend of having the opportunity to use
traditional domestic female skills of education and health-
care in a public context in response to religious ideals was
not confined in its attractivenss to religious founders, or
Catholics. Maria Luddy's research on women and philanthropy in nineteenth-century Ireland documents the great
numbers of lay women of different Christian denomin-
ations taken up in this movement.

All this serves to highlight the fact that the concrete
expression of a spirituality of social concern is intimately
enmeshed with the conditions of its socio-historical emergence. Contemporary feminist analysis of the nineteenth-
century women philanthropist's textual representation of
their work, by the researcher Kathryn Longden, has highlighted how these activities provided women with the rare
experience of acceptable, autonomous lives in the public
sphere. This acceptability was not of course universal and
women like Nano Nagle were, her contemporaneous biog-
rapher Bishop Coppinger reports, sometimes bitterly re-
viled. This effective fusion of the form of a spirituality of
social concern with the changing aspirations of women in
the nineteenth century raises the question of how a synergy
might today be generated.

*Towards Third-Generation Social Spirituality*

The realities of mass poverty, greater political desires on the part of women and the eighteenth-century resurgence of a spirituality of incarnation combined in a potent mix to fuel a socially concerned spirituality that captured the imagination of women in particular for more than 150 years. Each of the core ingredients in this mix has undergone profound redefinition, and their interconnections have been substantially altered in the past two decades. The future of a socially engaged spirituality depends on being able to offer a captivating imaginative reading of the socio-spiritual quest, akin to what those of the white martyrdom and philanthropy traditions offered to their respective audiences. I believe that there are three main movements involved in crafting an evocative, engaging expression of social spirituality for today.

Firstly, the spirit of the entrepreneurial culture in the current generation of young Irish business leaders needs to be creatively engaged. According to the recently published *Insights from the Winners Circle*, which gathers of the wisdom of winners over sixteen years of the Ernst and Young Entrepreneur of the Year Award, 'entrepreneurs are people who see what others don't see and they have the gift of looking at something differently; instead of seeing a glass of water, they see fluid dynamics'. The current difficulties regarding appropriate boundaries in ministry which are impacting so heavily on church confidence today have the real potential to quench the willingness to risk which entrepreneurship requires. Just as the desert struggles disheartened the Exodus wanderers, and the tossing boat terrified the companions of Jesus, tempting each to return to the comfort of the familiar, now may be the time to go travel more deeply into the unknown.

Historians of Irish women's religious history, like Rosemary Raughter, have noted that the weakness of hierarchical structures within eighteenth-century Catholicism

allowed women who wanted to integrate spiritual quest-
ing and social concern considerable latitude. In Ireland we
are emerging from one of the most seamlessly hegemonic
periods for Irish Catholicism. In such a situation it is inevitable that there is a lack of familiarity with that spirit of
religious entrepreneurship that characterised the eigh-
teenth and early nineteenth centuries. The spirit of entrepreneurship has been a key ingredient in recent economic
development and it will be necessary to engage this newly
emerging national trait if creativity in the service of religious vitality is to be released. By whatever means possible, a surfacing of the dreams held within individuals for
the future of a socially-engaged faith needs to happen.
Practical encouragements for the incubation of these ideas
need to be put in place by anyone with the means to do so.

That generation of religious entrepreneurs in the field
of social concern who emerged in Ireland after the Second
Vatican Council have not been replaced by another generation. Where is the missing generation? Have some of the
dynamics that once surrounded the inheritance of land,
which were so well portrayed in *The Field*, passed into the
realm of religion? If this had happened in industry, the
arts, politics or any other section of Irish life all would
recognise that the effects would be disastrous. The future
vitality of a spirituality of social engagement, depends on
a paradigm shift where the emerging culture of entrepreneurship may be creatively engaged, just as women's
changing social roles provided the fuel for the women religious social innovators of a previous generation.

Secondly, there will be a need to reflect deeply on those
religious movements of social concern, particularly in
Europe, that have captured contemporary imagination.
Nano Nagle saw that much could be learned from what
already worked elsewhere. Becoming familiar with initiatives that have already broken the soil and manifest the
first shoots of a new generation of social spirituality serves

to nurture hope and confidence. Reviewing them will not, however, replace the hard task of writing a new recipe that draws on those ingredients that suit locally, and discarding those that do not.

A striking feature of the contemporary expressions of social concern is the transition away from a focus on *doing* to *being*. A movement like L'arche epitomises this turn in spirituality. The quality of relations between persons is coming to replace the quantity of projects being undertaken. While great social challenges such as extensive poverty, homelessness and hunger still exist, what is perhaps more evident today is the destructive energy destroying the soul of humanity, that is manifest in violence, in war and in acts of personal and social destruction. An inability to allow another to be different and unfamiliar fuels these destructive forces. A new frontier awaits those who have the courage to arise and go. The invitation is to intentionally engage difference, to sit with others long enough to really hear their story as they wish to tell it. If walking was the key metaphor for the outgoing generation of spirituality, listening may become the image that captures a key mode of being in the new era.

In the second generation of social concern the text of Luke 4:1-3 acted as an anthem. Bringing the good news to the poor and proclaiming liberty to captives captured the imagination and inspired heroic action. Today it may be the triple introduction to this activity in the Lucan text that focuses the call to social concern. There it is evident that the actions are an outward manifestation of Jesus' attentiveness to and trust in the still small voice of the Spirit whispering deep within the realities of his life and times. Throughout the ministry of Jesus this disposition of attentiveness is his primary mode of ministry. He sits and spends time in conversation with another, listening, attending, learning and responding respectfully. The conclusion of the listening conversation with the woman at the

well in John's gospel witnesses powerfully to the personal
and social impact of such deep listening

A final reality that new movements of social concern
must engage is the possibility of extending into generations after their initial foundation. We saw above that the
powerful dynamic of female philanthropy in the 19th century cannot be adequately accounted for by simply focusing on the personal vocations of the women who founded
groups that continue to follow their inspiration to this day.
The movement of social concern that their lives incarnated
drew its power and energy from its effective capacity to
express the deepest aspirations of women in that era.

Events of global dimensions, such as the United Nations
Women's Conference in Beijing, are bringing about the
most fundamental shifts in the consciousness of women.
The Nano Nagle or Margaret Aylward of this generation is
faced with being able to intuit the shape of emerging
feminine consciousness. If gospel-inspired movements of
social concern, having the liberative impact on peoples'
lives of the mass health and education movements initiated
by women of previous generations, are to come into being,
a radical change in the culture and forms of women's religious life will be a pre-requisite.

Several hundred women in Ireland have walked away
from the current incarnation of the spirit of social concern
as it is being expressed in women's congregations today.
Many still experience a restless seeking for a better form of
expression of what drew them to these congregations in
the first place. Mary Magdalene stood by the cross of
Jesus, followed to the tomb where he was buried, and was
returning with spices to anoint Jesus' body when she was
confronted by his risen presence. In staying close to those
who have experienced the death of the old movements of
social concern, and going with them to where they lie in
wait for the new, the insight for another wave of life-giv-
ing movements of social concern may be born.

# CHAPTER EIGHT

# Life Coaches and the Spiritual Exercises

*Laurence Murphy SJ*

Many people reading these pages will know something of the Spiritual Exercises of St Ignatius but may never have heard of 'Life Coaches'. Aboodi Shaby, president of the International Coach Federation in the UK, reckons that there are about five hundred life coaches in Britain which means that there are upwards of thirty thousand people involved in life coaching in that country. He himself coaches about fourteen clients, spending many hours on the phone with them each week and keeping in touch via e-mails. 'I'm not a guru, I'm not a magician, but I am keeping people on track' he says. Life coaches help you assess your life now and then work out how to change it to the way you want to be in the future. Life coaching is a bit like its sporting counterpart. The coach will assist you in working out your goals, then help you to formulate a plan of action, encourage you to make progress and get on to you if you fall behind.

Gerry O'Donovan, originally from Bantry, is a life coach who works with trainees at the Life Coaching Academy in Portsmouth. He comes over to Ireland to host training sessions for Irish participants. He will readily admit that their techniques are based on the world of Olympic sports and has no doubts that if you were to question winning athletes about success, they would give a prominent place to their coach. The people who go looking for help from a life coach are more likely to be concerned about buying a house, help in setting life goals, improving personal relationships, getting on in business or even being a better parent at home.

To find out more about what actually goes on at one of O'Donovan's training courses, Susan Grey attended a session in England. Later she reported her experience in the *Irish Times*: 'The first task of a life coach is to listen.' According to her, listening is a skill we have forgotten in this busy world. We tend to half-listen, already preparing a witty reply as we listen. Frequently we filter what we hear through our own experience and jump in with solutions which may have worked quite well for ourselves but are in fact quite inappropriate for the person struggling to express himself or herself. The good life coach has learned to listen, listen and listen. They are instructed never to give advice but to help individuals find their own solutions by giving them time and space to think them through. One of the techniques used by the life-coach in helping clients is to ask what are called incisive questions. These 'cut through the obstacles that tend to hold people back: fear, procrastination, mental barriers, lack of clarity, lack of self-discipline.' A life-coach might stir up the client's desires by asking: if you were not afraid in this situation what would you do ? If you knew your children were taken care of in all aspects, what would you do with the rest of your life? Aided by the prodding of such incisive questions, people can be helped to clarify what they really want to do with their lives. Put another way, 'life coaches are concerned with helping their clients to crystallise their dreams into reality'. Usually they can do this better than friends and relatives because they don't bring their own agenda with them; by their training they can really listen and by their experience they have learned how best to help others.

In this more fragmented, more complex world with its new needs, Kathleen Fanning, an expert in time management with the Institute of Public Administration, coaches people how to manage that most precious commodity, their time. 'People want more control over their lives. Even opting to do a course in time-management is a recognition that there is a problem.' In an interview last year she gave practical advice on how to take more control over one's life: 'Knowing what you want is crucial ... deciding what is urgent as opposed to important, understanding the difference between maintenance and progress.' Make choices, then decisions and know yourself, sums up her advice.

The reader may well ask what has all this to do with the Spiritual Exercises. Helping others in a professional way has become a growth point in our world today. No mention has been made of the growth in counselling, psychotherapy and psychoanalysis. It is enough to look at the shelves of our bookstores to be struck by the number of self-help books. One thing is evident in our contemporary Ireland: many people are looking for help from sources outside themselves. While some are able and willing to pay generously for such help, the majority of people depend on what help is offered to them by the state or by voluntary bodies of one kind or another. Others still depend on a helping presence from a friend or a relative. Reflecting on the work of life coaches, there seems to be some overlap in their goals and even methods (like providing time and space, knowing what you want) with the work of those giving the Spiritual Exercises. Clearly there are significant differences. However, I believe we can learn from each other. Men and women desire to take more control of their own lives, to bring a self-imposed order into the disorder which threatens and at times succeeds in destroying families, careers, businesses, institutions and human life itself.

The Spiritual Exercises of St Ignatius Loyola are primarily to help men and women. Obviously they are not the only way nor are they the best way for many. In fact this Basque soldier-turned-mystic considered that he could offer nothing better to help persons. A paraphrase of their subtitle may assist the reader to know what is being re-

ferred to: these Spiritual Exercises are to help people take
more control of themselves by bringing order into their
lives through coming to decisions without being swayed
by disordered attachments. The small book of the Spiritual
Exercises consists of notes taken during his own conversion and added to later. Their goal is achieved by 'doing
exercises', not by reading the book or attending lecturers
about them. In order to do exercises, there must be someone who gives them or monitors the one doing them. In
what do these exercises consist? Their author says that
they are every way of preparing people to come to an
inner freedom which will permit them to find out a direction of their lives and one which is in keeping with the
desires of a loving God.

To 'do the Spiritual Exercises' is to go through a process
which will engage the whole person, physically, mentally,
psychologically and spiritually. At the very centre of this
process is the action of God in the person and more specifically God acting on the affectivity of the person. At a recent seminar on 'Ignatian spirituality and affectivity' the
principal speaker began by saying: 'Ignatius of Loyola
constantly instructs the one doing the Spiritual Exercises
to feel, to taste, to sense, and in this he is drawing on his
reflective awareness of his own affective experience.' As
Michael Ivens points out in his commentary on the
Exercises, the Spiritual Exercises are meant to lead to the
conversion of one's affectivity. In this way the drama of
our desires is central to the journey of the one doing the
Exercises.

Ignatius was no innovator as regards the Christian content but he adapted traditional spirituality and moulded it
into a unique synthesis with an underlying Christian an-
thropology. Many adaptations of these Exercises are possible to suit the needs and capacities of the individual. In
their fullest format they consist of four 'weeks' flowing
into each other, following a certain direction like a river

finding its way through valleys and plains to the sea. There is no need here to enter the debate as to whether they are designed primarily to lead to a decision or meant rather as a school of prayer and discernment. It seems they are both but will tend more in one or other direction depending on the person doing them. From the text itself the movement leads towards a decision for a new way of life or for change in one's way of living.

The person of Jesus Christ is at the very centre of the experience of the Spiritual Exercises. The kind of prayer suggested consists in contemplating (with the help of the affective-arousing imagination) the mysteries of the life of Christ. What happens here is no fantasy exercise nor just a recalling of an event two thousand years ago. Rather is it the re-enacting of the mystery itself, here and now, as the person prays. Here and now, Christ is born, heals, cures, preaches, raises to life and the person contemplating is called to identify with Christ and his mission.

'The entire process, as Ignatius conceived it, is guided and sustained by grace. But grace does not achieve its effects without active participation and engagement of the self. There are certain characteristics of the process which stem from activation of the ego. Our Lord provides such a rich source of aspects for imitation that the person must select. Selection will be partially determined by psychological factors in cooperation with and under the guidance of grace. From this point of view, identification with Christ is a very flexible concept, and its realization in various souls will follow highly individualized patterns.'[1]

During the 'weeks' of the Exercises when the mysteries of Christ's life are being contemplated, a question can be asked which is relevant to the subject matter considered in these pages. In these personal encounters with Christ in prayer, which Christ am I meeting ? Is it the Christ who is

1. W. W. Meissner, SJ, *To the Greater Glory – a Psychological Study of Ignatian Spirituality*, Marquette University Press, 1999, p 175.

in the scriptures or the Christ who is in the eucharist or the
Christ in my neighbour or Christ in nature or Christ in
history. In other words am I meeting the total Christ? Is it
possible that I am focusing on one aspect of the Risen Lord
while forgetting the other presences of Christ in my life?
'Lord, when did we see you hungry or naked or in prison?'
is by no means a new query. Christians throughout the
world have come to understand better in recent decades
the inseparability between the love of God and the love of
neighbour. At the same time we have started to grasp better the relationship between charity and justice. Slowly but
surely it is dawning on us that the very survival of the
planet which we humans inhabit is threatened where the inseparability of charity and justice is ignored.

As far back as 1971, the Synod of Bishops spoke of the
pursuit of justice as a constitutive part of the gospel; the
32nd Jesuit General Congregation spoke of the promotion
of justice as an integral part of the service of faith and
evangelisation. The social teaching of John Paul II has continued to develop and underline the commitment of the
church to social justice. Few persons have understood
more clearly the relationship between love of God and social
justice than Father Pedro Arrupe, former Superior General
of the Society of Jesus. In one of his last public addresses
before his stroke in 1981 he wrote these telling words:

'Charity has a social dimension, deriving not only from
the universality of charity but also from man's social condition. Charity on a merely personal basis is not enough.
In a world like today's, which is growing more and more
socialised, where people find themselves caught in the
mesh of socio-economic and political structures of every
sort, charity has to be understood and put into practice on
a social scale as well ... It (charity) aims precisely at improving those structures on which depends the welfare of
groups who have particular needs and wants.'[2]

2. Pedro Arrupe, SJ, *Rooted and Grounded in Love*, Conference read at the
*final session of the Ignatian Course in Rome, February 1981.*

Influenced by the social teaching of the church, but perhaps more by an awareness of their own shortcomings in this area, the Jesuits organised a summer programme of insertion to provide an experience of social injustice. The programme, called 'Companions for Justice', recognised a principle which is central in Ignatian spirituality: the significance of experience which touches our affectivity. 'There is knowledge and knowledge. To know about the weight under which people live their lives is one thing. To experience that weight, to have the imagination which allows accurate empathy, supposes not only knowledge about but also a real and developing relationship.' The programme served a useful purpose in that it provided an experience that could be reflected on individually and in a group. Truly it was an experience of spirituality and social theology. Twenty years later such experiences are part of any truly Christian formation programme.

In its Constitution, *The Church in the Modern World*, the Vatican Council wished to avoid any form of dualism which, following a Greek tradition, thought of the human person mainly as a composite of two substances, body and soul, united with each other. This rather bald statement makes this clear: 'Though made up of body and soul, the human person is one.'[3] However, from our past we have inherited dualistic habits of thinking which can have enormous and practical consequences. As David Lonsdale writes: 'We recognise or create distinctions between different dimensions of life, persons, objects or the world and then proceed to examine and discuss them separately, in isolation from each other and from the greater whole of which they are apart. We divide spirit from body, men from women, the inner from the external world, the personal from the social ... and we find it difficult to escape a tendency to assume that one of these pairs is superior to the other, to set them in opposition to each other and to

3. *Gaudium et Spes*, n 14.

treat the supposedly inferior with hostility.'[4] This tendency
is evident in trying to find the place in Ignatian spirituality
for a search for social justice as a demand of the gospel. For
those working directly in giving the Spiritual Exercises,
the inevitable attention given to the individual person can,
at times, run the risk of neglecting the social nature of the
person. Indeed, Ignatian discernment itself necessarily
focuses on the personal needs, desires and movements occurring within the individual. 'Some approaches to Ignatian
prayer and spirituality have a one-sided emphasis on personal, psychological and emotional well-being … The danger occurs when our engagement in Ignatian spirituality
does not integrate "inwardness" with, for example, socio-
political dimensions of life in prayer, reflection, spiritual
direction or discernment.'[5] The attraction of following
Christ today is the more powerful when the total Christ,
spoken of earlier, is constantly kept before our eyes. On the
other hand, for those working more directly for social justice there is the inevitable risk of disappointment, sense of
failure and intolerable frustration, if the person is not
deeply rooted through personal prayer in the mystery of
the death and resurrection of Christ.

With this new emphasis on the unity of the human person, attention needs to be drawn also to the unconscious as
a factor in any discussion of human behaviour and motivation. Throughout the Spiritual Exercises, it is evident that
Ignatius, while not having the tools and concepts of a post
Freudian culture, was nevertheless aware of the influence
of this hidden dimension operating in persons' desiring to
love God while seeking greater freedom from inordinate
attachments. If one accepts that there is in the human
person, a dialectic between conscious and unconscious
motivations, then the old dichotomy (either conscious-

4. David Lonsdale, *Eyes to See, Ears to Hear, An Introduction to Ignatian Spirituality*, Darton, Longman & Todd, London, 2000. p 206 et seq.
5. Ibid.

and-free, concerned with sin and virtue, or pathological-and-unfree, devoid of responsibility) no longer helps. There is need of a new, intermediate category inclusive of persons with unconscious motivations which are normal and not pathological but which nevertheless can and do introduce disorder into human lives. It is this reality of 'bias' (as Lonergan would call it) which is experienced by individuals, by groups, by countries, and is present today on a global scale, that runs contrary to the loving designs of a compassionate God, who loves all creation but who in Jesus Christ has shown a preferential love for the poor and oppressed.

The are many ways leading to God; there are many spiritualities. The spirituality spoken of in this chapter can lead persons to become 'contemplatives in action.' 'Contemplative' means rooted in a profound gratitude to God for what is, seeing all as gift and going beyond the gift to the giver who is God. 'In action' means showing the same effective concern for God's creation and God's people as God does. The challenge for Christians is to live holding both these dimensions together. The ability to do that is itself a gift of God to be continually asked for.

Clearly there has been an explosion of interest in 'spirituality' and in self journeying in these last few decades. The school of life coaching fits into this cultural context as do many of the surprisingly spiritual approaches now encouraged in the world of business.[6] Many of these paths are shy about God and sometimes downright allergic to Christianity. It is in this environment that the flexible skills of the Spiritual Exercises can find new life. Here is a Christian pedagogy, which with the help of a spiritual guide or coach, can integrate all that is best from the more secular developments that have come to the fore in recent times. The more spirituality can interact with the other sciences, the truer it will be to God, the Author of life, the giver of all blessings and gifts which descend from above.

6. Cf. Catherine McGeachy, *Spiritual Intelligence in the Workplace*, Veritas, Dublin, 2001.

# CHAPTER NINE

# Spirituality for Development for the Poorest

*Seamus O'Gorman SJ*

### a. Sonia Goes for gold

When I think of a spirituality up to the challenge of the way our world is, I often think of a phrase a journalist used of Sonia O' Sullivan's effort to win the gold medal in the 1992 Barcelona Olympics. Evoking that glorious moment when she broke to the front coming around the final bend, he wrote that the whole of Ireland got up off its 'collective arse and roared Sonia on'… 'go on…'. I laughed out loud when I read it, struck by its brilliant capturing of an event. I had watched the race in a pub, and that did happen. As Sonia burst into the lead, within sight of the line, all of the people around me did find it within them to leave the calm, cushy, comfy, relaxed place where they had so casually and relaxedly placed their backsides.

In spiritual contemplative mode there is so much about human life that is precious and fascinating. Yet one of the things that has often fascinated me most is what makes us get up off our 'arses'. Why did we all get up that day, and so many other days when Sonia runs? Why did a whole society – the young, the old, men and women, the rich, the poor, the religious, the atheists, the sports fanatics and the sportingly challenged, the left wingers and right wingers, the Dubs and the others … everybody – or at least so many people it didn't seem to matter – make the huge effort of detaching their backsides from their seats to leap to cheer Sonia on? What did she do to us that had the power to get us to rise up, to jump forward, to get involved? I particularly like the image because in a gentle kind of way it catches us out as Irish people. There is a certain honest ir-reverence in naming where we actually were positioned: sat back on our arses. And it somehow gets at where we often seat ourselves, as sceptical if not cynical spectators of the dramatic events of life and of history's becoming. We sat there with our self-protective 'ah sure she won't do too much, ah sure don't expect too much'. But that slightly col-lectively defensive attitude, that smug indifference was not so sturdy that it could not still be snapped through if something dragged us out of it.

The work I have been involved in over the last number of years, working as part of a Jesuit international network [JDRAD] involved in the campaign for third world debt reduction often makes me think of that journalist's phrase. Working with people to achieve a cancellation of unpayable third world debt so that some of the poorest people in the world have some chance of a life worth living, I often find myself wondering what it would really take to get us 'up off our arses' to do something about it. What would need to happen so that when the opportunity arises – as I be-lieve God makes sure it does – in your and my life that we would be ready as individuals, as groups and as a country to do what we can to feed the hungry and bring good news to the impoverished? What needs to happen so that the few who we easily blame for maintaining the present dis-order of things would find themselves without our tacit approval?

When I consider what happens to us watching Sonia, I think it is possible to identify three key elements which are involved – identifying, supporting, and seeing an end line – and which need to be present in a spirituality that sus-tains real commitment to God's commitment to justice on earth for the majority poor.

## b. The Irish go for development

### i) Identifying with the distant poor

We cheer for Sonia, as she strides out for gold, because she is one of our own. When you think about it, it's funny that that comes to be. Few of us know her, but somehow we end up being able to identify with her. Back in 1992 it must have been her Irish singlet, and the fact that the comment-ator picked her out while ignoring all the others.

To be affectively and in turn effectively moved by the poverty of the poorest millions of people in our world we need something similar. If we are not born amongst them, if their problems are not our problems, we need someone to point them out, to get us to take notice of them. The gospel picture of Jesus of Nazareth makes very clear that he made the desperate plight of the poor central to what he went on about when talking to people. Presuming his sincerity in going on about the poor, the only justification for the apparently platitudinous promises he made to the poor – about good news, about the kingdom belonging to them – was that he actually believed that deep down what God was at was working to bring about a world where the cry of the poor would be heard, and heard in such a way that all of us who create society would make responding to their needs our no 1 priority.

Thanks to the efforts of many – even of *Sky News* – it's hard not to know that there are millions of people in our world whose daily life involves a horrific struggle for sur-vival – for food, for water, for shelter – most of us in twenty-first-century Ireland could hardly imagine experiencing in our worst nightmares. But it's not enough that the far off poor are pointed out. Awareness is a necessary beginning in most spiritual searching but it is a dangerously insuffi-cient end point. The key thing is that we somehow have to be able to identify with them, to feel touched and moved by their plight. For that to happen, I think we need to let ourselves connect with their lives. The sad truth is that it is very easy to avoid doing this. Rather than learning to identify with our suffering sisters and brothers, we can clutter our lives with so much that we distance them from the heart of our lives. We very easily allow ourselves think they, the poorest people on the earth, the ones for whom old age begins at thirty, are different. They live far away, very few of them are white. Such accidental features can undermine how much we really consider them to be fellow human beings.

To my mind, almost worse still is that we happily take the mental escape route of believing that the way they experience poverty and death is very different to how we do. Many Irish people seem to know auntie 'Sr Marys' or uncle 'Fr Toms' who work in the Third World, and who think the people are 'absolutely wonderful, and so happy and joyful, and so spiritual, and indeed so grateful to the missionaries and all of us who send them money', that in some sort of way maybe the whole poverty thing isn't humanly that serious after all, 'and sure aren't they saved from the hustle and bustle of our busy, capitalist, consumerist lives?' From the short couple of years I worked in Zambia I saw that there is something tremendous and terribly humbling about the enormity of spirit of many people who suffer the daily crucifixion of poverty. However, I will always remember the violent tears of a young mother who sat beside me in the car as I drove her home. Her daughter had died from a sickness we would easily treat. For me it remains a stark reminder of the uncomfortable fact that they are equal to us in that they suffer no less than us the loss of each cherished life. Admiring what is good in the world of the poor should never become complacency about what it is to be poor.

It is difficult emotionally to learn to identify with the struggles of far off people. But, just as many of us end up identifying with the ups and downs of our favourite soap characters, it is possible to carry the poor as part of the

stuff of our daily life. God provides different concrete
steps that are open to all of us: for some it may be spending
a holiday volunteering in a poor country; for others it
might be to go and work there for a longer period of time;
for others again it can involve joining a solidarity group or
helping in some fundraising; for others it can simply mean
reading about what happens there before reading the
day's TV pages; for others it can just be noticing the presence of those whom God never forgets when you place
yourself before God. By building on our precious God-
given capacities to remember people we have met, to include them and their reality in our prayer, and to imagine
the limited possibilities of life being offered to them in
some way, the far away and remote reality of third world
poverty can find its way to become part of the story of our
lives.

ii) Supporting the poor
A first step then in developing a spirituality which addresses the reality of global poverty is to allow our hearts
and minds to be in some way hooked: either by the reality
of the affliction of the truly poorest people in our world; or
possibly by the awesome mystery of their dignified struggle to live life, to give them a space in our lives. So that this
can mature it seems that we need to find a way of allowing
it to be expressed in our lives. After all, the road to the ob-
scene levels of poverty we tolerate in a world of plenty is
paved with feelings of pity. The most beautiful feelings,
whether of compassion, tenderness, rage about injustice,
no matter how sincerely felt, simply die if we fail to honour these impulses through giving them adequate life enhancing expression. We have to gently get over indulging
ourselves in paralysing pity for the poor, and find some
way of making an engagement with active support of their
struggle for life, part of our lives. John Paul II put this very
strikingly when he wrote of the related idea of solidarity,

'This then is not a feeling of vague compassion or shallow distress at the misfortunes of so many people, both near and far. On the contrary, it is a firm and persevering determination to commit oneself to the common good; that is to say to the good of all and of each individual, because we are all really responsible for all.'[1]

Of course, many of us, as generous people, feel there is so little we can do with this wider responsibility. Global poverty is so vast, it has been around for so long. It is all so complicated, and so many worthwhile and good initiatives seem to lead to so little real progress. There are plenty of problems in our own country, such as homelessness or violence in Northern Ireland. In addition, modern life is so complex and so busy between work and family commitments it can often seem impossible to conceive of having any time to get involved. It can't be denied. There are difficulties in supporting the cause of development. So many of us end up a little dispirited perhaps, but in some way rationalising that 'we don't do third world poverty, it's not our thing.'

But when we have really learned to identify with the joys and hopes, the needs and concerns of the poor, I think it is often surprising to find a wide variety of ways to support the struggle for development, which can be appropriate to our skills and position in life. Just imagine that we set the standard for what we can do by what we would do if our own children, lovers or parents were faced with some sudden catastrophe. In such moments we discover untapped levels of our humanity, and how much all of us are actually capable of stretching ourselves to do no less than the impossible for others. If something of the generosity of the human spirit which shines in care for our own sick and grieving could be redirected towards the poorest, the man-made political and economic structures which block development would collapse.

---

1. John Paul II, *Solicitudo Rei Socialis*, 1987, 38.

In a country where more and more people take up
hobbies – learning to repair furniture, or how to dance –
any one of us, for example, can choose to make doing
something to reduce world poverty, during some period
or over the whole of our life, a certain priority in our life.
At a most basic level anyone can choose to do a course on
development issues, to read about it in papers, magazines,
the web, or to follow relevant news stories on the TV. If we
can find space for *Coronation St, Fair City*, or *Big Brother* in
our imaginary world, surely it is not beyond us to create
space to see and hear the stories of the real but broken
world.

At another level, it is of course possible to make direct
financial contributions to organizations, groups and projects which you believe are making a real effort to fight
poverty. This is a vital, direct and very tangible way of
translating feelings of vague compassion into real action.
Allowing your contribution to some organization to be another one of those standing orders you pay as part of life
with as much regularity as the ESB bill, or the phone bill,
or the weekend away, can be a way of affirming your sustained commitment to the redistribution of income necessary so that the poorest can live. It is also a way of giving
tangible witness to the fundamental Christian belief that
the goods of the earth are primarily intended for all the
people of the earth, with the implication that the wealth
we possess is under a social mortgage. Such direct action
can also have the advantages of immediate contact, where
you can be sure of fairly direct results and also of the satisfaction of knowing that even relatively small contributions
can be turned into real life-saving achievements.

While a very worthwhile and valuable way of being involved and expressing support in a meaningful way, there
are some dangers that the voluntary distribution of our
surplus cash to Third World projects can be somewhat
counterproductive in terms of achieving the real ends for

which we donate. Responding to direct and urgent needs is a vital task. It is not justifiable to wait till sufficient structural change has occurred and global income is distributed in such an equal way that such contributions are no longer needed. Nevertheless, it is crucial that personal financial contributions not be used as a buffer between us and the real call of the situation of the impoverished people. By giving a certain amount, even on a regular basis, we do not exhaust the potential contribution we can make to the more fundamental tasks of achieving poverty reduction. For real change to come about, not only for the few who benefit from the random lottery of international charity, it is vital that we engage as effectively as we can with broader and essentially political agendas which focus on the underlying causes of global poverty. The poverty of countless millions – not just the relatively few reached by our charitable donations – can only be reduced when citizens of the world force governments and political leaders to make it the priority issue.

One clear way of doing this is to get involved with people working for a more just global order. Throughout the world, there are a wide variety of groups working on the issues which can do with the support of the general public. There are groups and movements campaigning for increased aid, for trade reform, for human rights, for debt cancellation, for fair trade, and for a whole range of issues which are part of the challenge of putting an end to poverty around the world. In a world where we came to increasingly feel some genuine identification with the poor, it would be possible to imagine that people would realise that joining and actively participating in such groups and movements is a part of being human in a world which strives to destroy so much humanity. For those of faith it can become as natural a way of contributing to the coming of God's reign on earth as attending religious services or caring for one's children

iii) Focusing on the end line

The enthusiasm and drive to enable each of us to play our
role in the creation of a world order where the poor come
first, and to stick with the humble steps involved, is sustained by having the finishing line in sight, and the hope
that it can be reached. The knowledge that either victory or
loss is close by gives a sharpness and intensity to what we
put or do not put ourselves into. Sonia O'Sullivan seems to
find unknown and renewed reserves and energy when
within sight of the finishing line. So while we get up to
cheer her on because we identify with her, and because we
have got involved, it is also because we anticipate the
moment of celebration, the relief and rest of completing
the race, and the sheer joy of achieving the target.

The thought of reaching the finishing line – indeed that
it can be reached – is what keeps us going. Through God's
most precious gift of our imagination we need to conjure
up real images for ourselves of what that would mean in
the context of development: perhaps to sense the joy of the
hungry being fed, of the thirsty being given water, of
orphans being provided for. We need to break down the
seemingly enormous task of global development into
smaller and bigger pieces. A 13 lap race can't be won on
the first lap, but the possibility of winning can be greatly
helped if you make sure to get to the right place after a few
laps. None of us can get a grip on all of world poverty at
once. It is very easy to be so daunted and overwhelmed by
the scale of the task that we never get involved in the race
or disengage and allow life's other concerns and other images of happiness pushed at us to squeeze out a potential
desire to do what we can for development. Many painful
facts mean that ending world poverty can be dismissed as
an unattainable utopia. There is so much that needs to
happen and the forces of opposition apparently dedicated
to underdevelopment are so strong and interests are so
vested that it can seem beyond our reach. However, culti-

vating a clear sense of what can actually come about is vital to resist the temptation to believe this bad news.

With few resources, and even at little personal cost, quite extraordinary changes can be brought about. We need to be honest about that. What the few euro can do for us in terms of an extra pint, meal out, weekend away in Ireland with our high cost of living can be multiplied 10, 20 or 50 fold when we make it available in developing countries. In those countries it purchases so much more. But also by being made available in situations where the daily struggle is for life, money can truly bring joy in a way difficult for us to envisage. A little of our money can buy a lot of essentials. When we find ways of rechannelling the money which comes our way so that it is spent on basic food, medicines, shelter in the poorest corners of the world, we are drawn into the extraordinary miracle of creation, as it gives nothing less than life itself. At some stage in our lives most of us have the awesome privilege of holding a new-born baby, and the sense of being drawn into the mystery of the precious emergence of new born life. Holding one child in your arms, it becomes clear that every other child's equal potential to grow into human life is worth our generous support. Small money, money you'd hardly miss, can easily be used to create an opportunity for children to smile, to laugh, to taste all that the majority of us in the developed world take so for granted. Stretching our imagination can allow us get over the relatively minor matter that we may not be there to see the joy. But in fact in a way you can see it in the joy and happiness of seeing those you love being provided for, and remembering that what you are doing is directly allowing others to feel that.

These partial and more personal successes give us a hint of how much better things could be. They also importantly give us a taste of how much better and really human we would feel and so can be an important stimulus to imagining the bigger changes needed. The great success of the Jubilee campaign for debt cancellation was to unite so many thousands of different people all around the world in the push to achieve an end to the disastrous and senseless situation where money was flowing from the neediest and most desperate to the best-off nations of the world. Not everything has been achieved. There is still much to do but the conviction that people from around the world could be united as true sisters and brothers in saying no to unpayable debt being paid is part of what opens up the possibility of world changing efforts in the struggle to defeat poverty.

### c. Jesus goes for the Kingdom

When I pray I often wonder about Jesus and the kind of spirituality that fuelled his life, and why he ever got up off his arse and left his peaceful life in Nazareth, and above all why he headed up to Jerusalem. I am inclined to think there must have been many days in his subsequent years when he wondered why, and certainly his life did then raise a question of whether it was all worth it. Why did he do it? Could it be as simple as that he thought, or felt within his bones, that a completely different situation was not that far off for the people who most desperately needed it and so felt seduced into getting involved with it to the best of his ability. And so when he taught us to pray, maybe he hoped that we would come to glimpse that that is precisely the kind of life and world changing thing we commit ourselves to every time we mumble the words 'your kingdom come'.

# CHAPTER TEN

# Encountering the Stranger
# Finding the Good Samaritan in each of us

*Eugene Quinn*

*All God's people are equal*

I have had the good fortune to have met and shared time with a great number of people, from different, races, creeds, background and political affiliations, who continually force and challenge me to re-evaluate how I understand the world and our role in it. I have experienced the danger of judging people by their appearances and humbly having to admit later that my judgement had been rash and unfair. Labels can be dangerous because of the associations and images they conjure up. When we label a person or a group as strangers our opinion is being shaped even as we think it.

When we encounter a stranger, what motivates us? In my experience our actions will be motivated by what is in our hearts. If our fears predominate, then unsurprisingly we will look at those we do not know with fear and suspicion. On the other hand if love is the dominant motivation, we can recognise our shared humanity with the stranger. They have a family, a history and their own unique life's journey. They have hopes and dreams and needs. In other words, it is confirmation that we are all created equals by virtue of our human dignity. Christ, through his life and death, affirmed this fundamental equality. If we believe really in the equality of all people then their suffering and pain is a concern of ours. The radical equality that underpins the gospel message is embodied in communion, uniting all people in the Body of Christ.

## Fear and the Good Samaritan

The very notion of 'the stranger' often evokes fearful connotations in us. An image is conjured up of a shady and shifty person keeping to the shadows and bent on visiting evil upon unsuspecting persons. As children we are warned 'Don't talk to strangers', hinting at unspoken dangers from these anonymous individuals. The premise of the Good Samaritan story involves a personal engagement with the stranger and by definition with our fears. We have all experiences in our lives where we see a stranger in need; often our first reaction may not be for their welfare but rather for our own. In the world we live in we are conditioned by fears to automatically distrust that with which we are not familiar. Society propagates myths of predatory individuals who target would be 'Good Samaritans' due to their gullible nature. Thus when confronted with a person in need we are often assailed by uncertainties about the trustworthiness of their plea, the dangerousness of their appearance, our personal safety or perhaps a lack of belief in our ability to intervene helpfully.

Fear can be paralysing. It can also be real. There is always a risk in reaching out to the need of another. The risk is different for each individual. In the gospel story the Levite and the priest walked past the person in need. We are not told why. We are told that they crossed the road. This is a most human reaction. One way to avoid such a crisis of conscience is by avoiding direct contact altogether. Surely if either of these men had continued on the same side of the road it would have been much more difficult to have done nothing. Everyday in our cities we walk by strangers in need – the homeless, asylum seekers, addicts and many others on the margins of our society. Rarely do we feel comfortable. Even in our fear we are challenged by the injustice of their situation. We are aware that their reality is not a passing moment but a living nightmare. The Good Samaritan is a story of hope. It is an example to us, a vindication of love over fear.

## A life-changing encounter

The stranger comes in many guises. They may be somebody we do not know who enters our community. It may be people who are from a different country or have different beliefs or come from a different social class or simply look different. In a city it can be the myriad people who pass us by or whom we pass by on the street. In common they share the characteristic of being unknown and unfamiliar. Strangers may inspire both love and fear but more often it is fear. It is at the point of encounter that the relationship with the stranger changes. It has been critical to the direction of my faith journey.

My experience as a young professional of visiting families with the Saint Vincent De Paul shattered my comfortable worldview. I was unprepared for what I was to encounter. I saw firsthand the huge gulf between those who have and those who have not. I simply had to compare my own life with that of those I was visiting. They were two different worlds (in many respects it was like two different planets). I could afford gym membership, holidays abroad and to buy my own house. In their world I encountered the dangerous world of debt (not mortgages but moneylenders), structural unemployment, violence and substance abuse.

I asked myself how would I behave if I had not been born into a loving and supportive family environment, where any achievement no matter how minor was celebrated. An environment where any worries were soothed away with a kind word. How different would my life be if I had grown up in the harsh reality of an urban jungle with its associated social fragmentation and dislocation? How would I be perceived by my peers? It is easy to utter platitudes about self-help and extricating yourself from the poverty trap, but it is obvious that there are deep structural factors that act against this outcome. There are no easy answers to the deep inequities and social exclusion that divide Irish society.

There are real difficult questions for a Christian who lives in such a society.

There is so much judgement of people; of strangers who might rob our houses, might steal our cars or might attack us. So often we demand retribution and ever-harsher penalties without ever questioning why they do it. We judge very quickly. We react to the outcome of their actions while failing to ponder the causes. By benefiting from a system that excludes a significant proportion of our society, are we condoning it? Are we acquiescing to maintain a corrupt status quo that does not strive to enable all members of society to participate fully and equally?

An examination of education statistics reveals a shocking situation – one in four young Irish people leave school with no more than the basic compulsory education. It is no coincidence that the majority of this group comes from the poorest and most disadvantaged areas of Irish society. Education is a passport to employment and its absence by definition slams the door shut on many opportunities. Additionally, in trying to find employment people are subject to numerous unacknowledged prejudices regarding appearance, accent and address.

It is unpleasant to realise that prejudices are not the preserve of extremists but are unconsciously embedded across the whole spectrum of society. We all have numerous prejudices that are not articulated but subtly guide our actions. These prejudices are key to maintaining the status quo. An example may illustrate. Take an employer faced with two equal candidates but one has an address from a disadvantaged area and the other from a middle class area. It is likely that most employers will choose the latter, justifying their choice perhaps by the thought 'they will fit in better'. The truth is that it is discrimination. How do we reward an individual who triumphs in the face of disadvantage to be in a position to be employed? They find their employment opportunities limited by potential employers subtly discriminating against them by virtue of their ad-dress, an item over which they have little control. I find it challenging that I have a privileged position in Irish soci-ety by virtue of my birth (and not simply by the fruits of my own honest endeavour) and that conversely by the same arbitrary event a large number of people are excluded from the same society. It is no wonder Christ presciently observed 'The poor will be with us always'.

My faith required examination against these provoking and challenging questions, questions that go to the root of what my faith means. I realised that up until now it had rarely gone beyond the realm of the abstract, in reality in-truding little on my daily living. By doing nothing I was silently acquiescing in a system that polarised and divided Irish society. I had to acknowledge that, if my faith was going to be real, I could no longer go on blithely ignoring the reality of injustice and inequality. It was as if I discov-ered that my faith was not simply a set of rules of what *not* to do but more importantly was a call *to do*, discovering voc-ation so to speak! My faith had been set on a new course, a path that would lead me to change jobs, country and career.

## Living in a Strange Land

Perhaps the easiest way to understand what it feels like to be a stranger is to be one. I spent two years living and working in Bosnia. The word for foreigner is 'stranac', which translates literally as stranger. Apart from the usual dislocation of arriving in an unfamiliar place, the babble of an unknown foreign tongue adds to one's sense of bewild-erment. There is a great frustration in being unable to in-teract fully with other people. The language 'handicap' and the way you look single you out as different. You feel that you are getting the 'special' tourist price and that peo-ple are not always being honest with you, but there is nothing you can do about it. This helplessness gives a tiny insight into what life is like on the margins.

I am forever indebted to my Bosnian friends for their openness and hospitality, that this feeling of strangeness was only brief. Also, in Bosnia being a foreigner and a member of the international community automatically places you in a position of power. As a fieldworker on a Jesuit Refugee Services (JRS) assistance programme for children mine survivors and their families, I had responsibility for determining who received help and the extent of that assistance. The unequalness of the relationship is evident. I have always been struck when I visit families in need what an invasion and a humiliation it is for them to have to be dependent on strangers for assistance. Their private family space is forced by circumstances to be opened to people not of their choosing.

The Bosnian people are very hospitable. Even in their impoverished situation, often temporarily occupying the home of a person who was displaced in the war, and with a small and uncertain income, they will offer the visitor the best of what they have. Sharing coffee and the occasional *rakije* (a home produced brandy) restores equality to the relationship, affording them the dignity of hosts. The relaxed nature of drinking a coffee personalises the experience and enables a mutual exchange of stories and experiences. By getting some sense of my personal history, my homeland and my family background, a process of familiarisation and friendship was begun. The journey towards friendship transformed our initial mutual strangeness. Soon we could laugh together (usually at the expense of my language mishaps) and sometimes cry as we remembered the war and its associated sorrows.

People have often asked me was it difficult working with children mine victims. Without question it is not easy to witness children deprived of the use of their limbs. There is a possibility that being a mine victim can define them as people. The aim of our program was to aid our children inasmuch as we could to return to independent living. Friendship was an integral element. We worked with the whole family, not just the mine victim. The capacity of the mine victim to recover and re-enter society was inextricably linked with the family environment. Some parents, often ridden with guilt for what they perceive was their failure to protect their child, smothered them with love, in the process smothering their ability to rehabilitate. At the other extreme some parents rejected their child because their injuries meant they could no longer fulfil the dreams they had for them. The behavioural patterns of the children were determined as much from their injuries as from how they were treated subsequently in their families.

Hasib, a big strapping lad from up Vlasic Mountain, acted as if he had never lost his leg. He continued to work long hours on the family's mountainside farm despite the uneven terrain and absence of conveniences. He still played football, went to discos and hung out with his mates.

Benjamin, on the other hand, was brittle, angry and reclusive. His mother doted over him and suffocated him with her love. She treated him as different and special, probably harbouring an unacknowledged sense of guilt at what she perceived was her failure to protect her child. All of the initiatives we proposed to him he ultimately rejected. There was little we could do without first changing his family environment.

In Una Sana canton, a poor and remote rural area in northwest Bosnia where the war had been at its most fierce, Amir had lost both legs having stood on an anti-tank mine. His father lost respect for him because he could neither work the land nor produce an heir. Understandably this had profoundly affected his self-esteem. It was a wonderful moment in the Summer Camp when he was carried into the sea and to his amazement the buoyancy allowed him to be self-supported for the first time since he was injured. The sea had temporarily given him back his independence.

The beach experience had a tremendous affect on the children from our project. Many were initially afraid of togging out in their swimsuits because it would draw attention to their injuries. Being part of a group all of whom were injured freed them from the 'shame' of their deformity. Soon they were leaving literally a stack of leg and arm prostheses in their wake as they headed for the water. Those whose injuries were less serious carried those who could not walk into the water. For a short time their injuries did not distinguish them as different but rather were a source of unity and shared experience.

These and many other experiences in Bosnia altered how I perceived the world. I in no way intend to glorify their suffering simply because many of those who had suffered appalling injuries bore them with strength and dignity. It highlighted all the more the indifference of a watching world while this conflict was unfolding before our eyes. I questioned why I had done nothing. In this age of globalisation we were aware of the horrors in Bosnia. We watched aghast as the full extent of the horrors that were perpetrated was revealed: the mass rapes, concentration camps, the genocide and the ethnic cleansing. Unfortunately all we did was watch. On a personal level I was busy pursuing my career as an actuary as the war raged. I condemned myself for my indifference. I never lifted a pen in anger, never articulated my support in any meaningful political way. Generally people were too polite to talk about the hurt they felt by being left 'to fight it out'. Compare the response to September 11th. Little wonder that the people of Bosnia (and Rwanda and the innocent victims of countless other conflicts) might doubt that a human life is valued equally across this planet.

*Engagement is key*

Returning to our theme of the stranger and the Good Samaritan story, my reaction to the conflict in Bosnia when it was happening in the early to mid nineties was like that of the Levite or priest. My problem, like theirs, was not that I had done anything wrong but that I had done nothing at all. It can be argued that there are maybe fifty conflicts in the world at any given time, surely you can't hold yourself responsible for not getting involved with all of them. But to get involved in none of them, to ignore the poverty, the famine and the suffering of millions on the planet is wrong. Nobody said the gospel message was easy and without cost. But how we consider strangers, people who live beyond the shores of this cosy little island, is of vital importance in defining who we are as people. If we believe in equality then 'the suffering of the least of my brethren' is of the utmost concern to each and every one of us.

In the JRS mission statement the overarching aim is summarised in the phrase 'to accompany, advocate and serve the cause of refugees and asylum seekers'. The idea of accompaniment is key. This involves a personal engagement with those whom we serve, which enriches immeasurably the work we carry out. Oftentimes in Bosnia I pondered who was helping whom. As a westerner I would often allow myself to get fretful and stressed over the project delivery, needing a visit to a family to jerk me back to reality. Ironically, they, with all their problems and uncertainties, were better able to live in the present and to enjoy the moment. Perhaps they had learned from the bitter experience of the war not to take peace for granted. 'Polako!' they would say to me, which basically means 'chill' and take it easy. There was always time for coffee! One fellow-worker most accurately articulated the relationships with our families as an 'exchange of gifts'. We were bringing medical, material and legal help and in return we received friendship, spiritual help and the privilege of sharing their journey for a while.

In the end there are many lessons that we can learn from 'strangers' but it requires us to reach out personally. The courage of the Good Samaritan transformed a desperate situation into one in which both benefited. The gospel teaches us that the stranger does not have to be a foe but a friend. It is a triumph of love over fear.

# CHAPTER ELEVEN

# Social Justice, Why bother?
## The role of spirituality in social justice volunteering

*Patricia Higgins*

*'No one gives a f\*\*\* about me who isn't paid to do it.'*

This quote is from a young person who has spent time in prison. I have never met this person; their words were passed to me by someone else, but the phrase has stayed with me. It captures something of what I think volunteering has to offer which the market system fails to provide. Market forces constrain many to relating, at least in work, from within the context of a service-provider/ client relationship. The ability to genuinely care and respond to needs can be undermined, or at least affected, by the knowledge that the relationship is financially motivated.

The above quote captures the experience of such a relationship for the 'client'. He clearly felt the lack of freely-given care. 'Service-providers' too, can feel stymied by their professional roles. I now work with *Slí Eile*, an initiative of Irish Jesuits to provide faith and justice activities to 18-35 year olds, placing volunteers in part-time social-justice placements. A number of people who I have placed as volunteers have spoken of desire to be freer of the boundaries that they have to work within as teachers, solicitors or accommodation managers. They, too, want to be able to relate to people they work with differently. Volunteering allows them the chance to do that, though it requires its own set of boundaries. Care needs to be taken that both the volunteer and the people they volunteer with understand what they can reasonably expect of each other.

This chapter will explore what role spirituality plays in drawing people in to social justice volunteering and sustaining them in that involvement. I will begin by explaining my own understanding of social justice volunteering and spirituality. Drawing on my own experience of joining a JVC ( Jesuit Volunteer Communities) – a ten month fulltime volunteering program which combined work for social justice along with community, simple lifestyle and Ignatian spirituality – I will explain how, for me, spirituality acted as both the impetus to become a volunteer, and as the motivation to stay involved. Or in the words of the title, how spirituality was the reason to 'bother' and to 'keep on bothering'. I will highlight some of the key practical supports and insights which in my experience help to sustain volunteer involvement. Finally, I will offer some thoughts on the role of volunteering within the overall struggle for justice and how volunteering might fit into sustainable faith-based involvement in social justice, from a lay-person's point of view.

## Social Justice Volunteering

My experience of social justice volunteering within the JVC program was of working with and for people who are disadvantaged in Irish society today. I had the chance to choose from a list of placements all of which involved work with people on the margins, including children with disabilities, people living with HIV/AIDS, people affected by drug use, homeless people, refugees and asylum-seekers and people living in disadvantaged areas of the city.

I chose to spend my placement as a JVC volunteer in a community adult education project in a disadvantaged area of Dublin. The centre offered courses in meditation, drama, cookery, flower-arranging and other arts and crafts. My work involved helping to organize, advertise and host these courses, participating in the review and planning of the activities of the centre, networking with other community groups … and lots of just sitting and chatting to people who dropped in.

*Spirituality*

I understand spirituality as 'my relationship with God' and, for me, this was the key to allowing the experience of volunteering to have a real impact on me. As JVC volunteers, we were encouraged to reflect on the different experiences in our work that affected us – both the uplifting ones and the frustrating ones – and to be open to the notion that God might be saying something to us through them. This Ignatian idea of 'finding God in all things' was new to me. Being open to hear what God was saying through these experiences allowed for growth (not without a certain amount of struggle!) and appreciation of God's presence in my work. That made JVC volunteering different from other forms of volunteering that I had done before. With these there had been no means to process the range of emotions that could be stirred up, and the result had been a growing sense of frustration. The regular opportunities provided in JVC to reflect on the experience of work allowed me to acknowledge the frustrations before they became overwhelming, and to be more appreciative of the joys in the work.

*Why Bother – Spirituality and deciding to volunteer …*

The key motivation behind my decision to join JVC at the age of 24 was that I wanted to know God. I'd 'talked the talk' having been involved in a CLC (Christian Life Community) group for years, where I had reflected with other young adults on how to integrate the gospel into our daily lives. Now, I wanted to 'walk the walk'. I had a desire for more integrity between what I believed in and how I lived, and also a deeper sense of wanting to get to know and connect with God in a way that I hadn't managed to until then. I could see others who had this deeper sense of God and felt a mixture of envy and awe. I knew they were involved in their work with the disadvantaged primarily because of the passion they had for the gospel message. I

could see and hear the real life it gave them. I had some
sense that if I was prepared to risk working along with 'the
poor' that that might be a way to tap into the life and passion they had found.

For me that was a real risk. I had had few encounters
with people from disadvantaged backgrounds. I had a
whole complex of fears around reaching out; scared I'd
want to run away from the pain I saw, scared of getting
sucked into that pain of the people I was with, and yet also
being scared of rejection by them – scared perhaps most of
all of hearing 'What the hell are you here for? Go back to
your patronizing do-gooder middle-class roots.'

But the pull to know more of God and to know more of
where God wanted me to be was stronger than these fears.
I could no longer listen to and pray with the gospel and
say that gospel values were powerfully good. I had to find
some better way of putting them into practice in my life. In
college as an economics student I learnt that one of the
basic axioms upon which most modern economics was
based was that the utility (or satisfaction) of a person was
directly linked to their ability to consume goods and services. That seemed so obviously flawed. I'd wanted to
argue passionately that that was wrong. I felt strongly
that, beyond a certain point where needs are met, posses-
sions can clutter and choke. Now I felt a call to risk living
out of that belief by letting go of a path that was more con-
ventionally secure.

God had also been at the centre of my motivation to get
involved in previous volunteering work, in both school
and college. That, however, was more out of a sense that it
was something I 'should' be doing as a believer, than out
of any innate love for, or draw to, the work. I did have
moments of real connection with people, both the different
groups of people we worked with and other students, but
there was plenty of gritting my teeth and wishing the time
on whatever visit or outing I was on would come to an

end. Not surprisingly, I ended up fed up and burnt-out. The person who was guiding the CLC group I was then involved in suggested to me that God didn't operate using 'should'. He went further to suggest that 'should' could be a means of temptation; the most effective means of tempting a person who essentially wants to do good is not by tempting them to do nothing, but rather to do too much. This can draw them into a space where they give up, as I had done. The way forward was to accept it was ok to let go, take space and let what I truly wanted to do emerge in some way. And something about wanting to know God, wanting to engage with people in a real way emerged as the call. To respond I had to take a deep breath and trust.

*Why keep on Bothering –*
*Spirituality as a motivation to stay involved*
The phrase from Ephesians, 'so much more than we can ever ask for or imagine' (Eph 3:20), comes to mind when I think of how much I was given by God in return for that initial trust on my part.

> Catherine reached for my hand. She had tears in her eyes and a quiver in her voice. The other women gathered in that small kitchen in the basement flat murmured sympathetically as Catherine talked of it soon being her husband's first anniversary. A year on the pain was still there. This was a safe place to let it surface. I was sitting next to her and so the hand she'd reached for was mine. She squeezed my hand hard and I squeezed back, hoping that somehow that would help.

That happened when I was only two weeks in my placement. Even now, five years on, that immediately comes back as a really affecting moment; the awesome sense of being allowed in to the heart of someone's life. Having been there such a short time, I was in awe that someone would so readily reach to me for support. In some real way, for first of many times during that year, I was aware of God's presence in that place, with those women, around that oil-cloth covered table. I had volunteered in order to know God and the repeated opportunities to experience something of God's presence there was a very strong reason to stay involved.

### Key practical supports and insights

Looking back I can see that certain things were a real support in sticking with the volunteering: having a role in my placement, sharing with other volunteers, being given the chance to better understand root causes of disadvantage that we faced in our work, and learning to let go.

### Having a role

Having a clear role within the project I worked with offered the means by which to genuinely connect with people. Having something concrete to do allowed me to see beyond my fears and prejudices to the goodness and humanity of the people I met. As a Northerner who grew up having met hardly any Protestants despite living in a town where the population was 50% Protestant, 50% Catholic, I know something of the fear and prejudices that can breed when there is no chance for people to meet and get to know each other as real people. It was with a shock that I realised the same is true in Dublin for the disadvantaged and the better-off. Though I had friends from the area where I was working, I was still scared at the prospect of going to work there on my placements. The bad press that the place got had impacted on me, though I'd have been slow to admit it. I was scared of the reality of being on the ground and scared of how I'd be received. These fears could flourish where there are few naturally occurring opportunities for the 'advantaged' to meet the 'disadvantaged'.

Without that role the situation would have overwhelmed me. I realised this after seeing the reaction of a friend who walked with me to work one morning. Though normally very chatty, from the moment we entered the area I worked in, he went quiet. The path through the flats to the centre looked its worst with all the litter from the weekend strewn about. Only when we were in the centre itself did he speak. 'This is awful, how do you do it?' I realised my mind was focused on my 'to-do' list for the day – wash the floor, get the teabags and the milk, make such and such a phone call. I had a space from in which I could connect and hope to make a difference to the place little by little. He had no such role or space and so was floored by the impact of seeing the disadvantage so close.

### Sharing with other volunteers

Social justice volunteering is an expression of wanting things to be different and joining a fulltime program was a way to meet and engage with other people of like mind. I found the chance to share the highs and lows with the other JVC volunteers a real help.

### Input on causes of disadvantage

Within JVC we were given the chance to stand back from the 'coal-face' involvement of our work placements to try and better understand what were the root causes of the disadvantage we dealt with everyday. These inputs pushed the challenge to 'make a difference' beyond the time spent in placement, out into other areas of our lives, what we spent our money on, what we chose to get informed about, how we choose to vote etc. This was challenging, but ultimately, empowering. It allowed us to see the choices we could make in our lives to move further towards a more just and equal society.

*Letting go ...*
Learning to see the small steps I could take as an individual and so become more part of the solution than the problem was a healthy resolution of the 'control' dilemma I encountered as a volunteer. As with many people who are trained for jobs in the business world, I had been trained to problem-solve and to take control of situations that were my responsibility. A friend of mine, who works as an accountant, once heard a Jesuit speak of his work in an African refugee camp. His reaction to the presentation was, 'I don't know how he does that, facing into a situation he knows he can't fix.' The sentiment resonated with me. I quickly realised that, while there was some scope to plan the activities of the centre, there was no way I could hope to 'solve' any of the underlying problems. At that time I heard an advent reflection in which the efforts of John the Baptist were described as 'pouring oil and spices over rotten food. He was not the Christ. He could not change humanity.' There was a big challenge to let go of the need to achieve, solve, fix; a reluctant realisation that I did not *have* to solve it and that I could leave that to God. Without that belief in something bigger, that sense of not being able to make problems go away would have eroded my motivation to be there.

*Social Justice Volunteering within the overall struggle for justice*
Much of the injustice in our society today is built into our systems. Volunteering with people who are directly affected is one response, but one which will not by itself change the world we live in. Changing a whole system, as I mentioned above, can seem an impossible task. But I find huge comfort in thinking that Jesus' mission can also be seen in terms of 'changing a system'. He challenged the religious system of his day which kept people in a legalistic bind and fear of being unclean using a variety of strategies. One such strategy was of appealing to the atrophied parts of

people. He appealed to their imaginations and hearts through the use of simple powerful stories and this appealed to people's compassion and humanity, which had been deadened by legalistic religious observation.

As someone who works to encourage young people to volunteer on a parttime basis in social justice, I find the question of what is atrophied (or paralysed) in people today a good starting point in determining how to promote the opportunity to volunteer. What can be appealed to in people in order to engage them in the work of building the kingdom, of working to make our systems more just? What does our economic, political and social system in our world today not provide that volunteering could open up? It excites me that by offering people something in volunteering that the market system leaves atrophied, we could be working towards change at a bigger systematic level. And there's evidence to show that that can happen. The opportunity to reflect on questions thrown up by their experience of volunteering with the marginalised has led those involved to make changes in other areas of their life: in choice of careers, decisions on how to vote, and involvement in other forms of volunteering such as political lobbying and advocacy.

*Sustainable involvement in volunteering*
When I joined JVC, some people interpreted it as me taking my chance to 'do my bit' before returning to a life in the work that I'd done before. And the idea of having been there, done my bit for social justice and ticked it off the list of 'things to do in my life' certainly was attractive. In my more open and generous moments, though, I was hoping that JVC would open up a way of putting a commitment to social justice into practice beyond the end of the ten month period. While working as a volunteer, there was a very direct sense of being involved and committed. There can be a struggle after such a period to find a way to be com-

mitted to the same ideals. I find peace in the idea that, per-haps, as a lay person, I am called to 'cycles of involve-ment'. The experience of volunteering, for me, triggered a change of heart, to want things to be different with a greater passion. That has led to a sense of being drawn to further study, to better understand the situations of disad-vantage, training to improve my skills to address some of these, and being more involved at the level of lobbying and campaigning. Obviously, I can't do all of these at once. So while different people have different calls, it is also true that at different times in life, I may be drawn to different things. I may have to sacrifice the sense of being in touch on the ground in order to upskill, do other much-needed background work, or simply take time for other recreative things to restore my energy and enthusiasm. Reaching out is an element of Christian living but one that has to be pos-sible alongside people's other calls and commitments to work, family and other relationships.

# CHAPTER TWELVE

# Rediscovering Nature's Integrity

## *Niamh Gaynor*

They swim in circles all day long. Their six metre holding tank allows little room for anything else. Once they travelled thousands of miles from where they were born to spawn. But today, overfishing and pollution from industrial and agricultural effluent have rendered this journey even more arduous and numbers are fast dwindling. To meet consumer demand, increasing numbers are now bred and reared in tanks such as these. Their natural life-cycle, involving the remarkable journey from freshwater spawning grounds to distant oceans and back has now, for many, been broken.

The fate of the wild Irish salmon serves as a powerful illustration of the modern devaluation and destruction of the diversity of life and its mysteries. Traditionally the salmon was revered for its wisdom. The legend of Fionn Mac Cumhaill and the Salmon of Knowledge celebrates this. Atlantic salmon were admired for their strength and resilience in travelling from as far as the seas off Greenland to our rivers and lakes. Now their survival is threatened. Our response has not been to act to preserve their way of life, however, but rather to preserve and commercially develop a food resource. What was once revered and sacred has now become a mere commodity. The respect and awe we once felt is lost. Salmon have become a commercial resource like any other, to be exploited for our own consumption.

The salmon's fate is but one illustration of the impact on our planet of our ethnocentric, exploitative approach to its mysteries. We are destroying not only our natural resources base, but life itself – the earth, the waterways, the species they nurture. This chapter explores our relationship with this life around us – how this, following different traditions, has evolved/disintegrated over time. The chapter argues that we, in sharing a deeper spiritual value with this life, are part of it. And so, when continually looking inwards seeking to serve individual, ethnocentric needs, we harm the life systems of the planet, and we ultimately harm ourselves. The latter part of the chapter argues that current economic and political systems, together with our individual actions, focused inwards on the individual, are accelerating this damage. These will only change through a fundamental shift in values where we respectfully take our place, alongside and equal to all other life, in a more integral society, and where we choose our actions accordingly.

## 1. OUR PERCEPTIONS OF NATURE

The causes of the current crisis are inextricably linked to how we perceive the earth. Do we see it as something sacred, something encapsulating a deeper value also within us, or do we see it as something separate from ourselves, a spiritless resource base to be used for our benefit? Do we appreciate that nature's complete spirit and complexities lie beyond our narrow realm of understanding or do we feel nature is 'out there' for us to dissect, analyse, comprehend, and utilise?

### 1.1 Traditional Perceptions of the Integrity of Nature
Our perceptions are strongly influenced by our cultural and religious traditions. In many traditional societies different elements of nature possess their own spirits. The

Sincere thanks to Fr Sean McDonagh for his insights and guidance in preparing the preliminary section of this text.

sacred/spiritual is not seen as something apart, but as an integral element diffused through nature around us. This is the perception among many peoples around the world. Keri Hulme, in her novel *The Bone People*,[1] vividly evokes the Maori earthbound spiritual tradition, whilst Bruce Chatwin's *The Songlines*[2] explores the complex relationships between human nature and the shaping of the land. Our own Celtic tradition here in Ireland, where God's presence was always mediated through some finite earthly matter, strongly echoes this. Traditional religious practices in many cultures often centre around attracting or repelling the spirits. The agricultural Bariba of Northern Benin for example,[3] neither plant nor harvest without calling on the earths' spirits to aid them. A solitary tree standing in the middle of a cleared field is a common sight. The tree contains an important spirit and so can never be cut down. This holistic view of spirituality informs a reverence and a respect for nature where nature is not seen as a commodity to be owned and exploited, but rather as a companion to be nurtured. The Bariba employ an expression: 'The land was not given to us by our grandparents, it was lent to us by our grandchildren.' This illustrates their perception of their role as custodians of something permanent to be respected, rather than exploiters of a shorterm resource.

## 1.2 Western Philosophy Introduces a Duality

The rise of the great religious and philosophical traditions in the West signaled an important change in the way Western cultures viewed the spiritual, the world, and human beings. The Greek philosophical tradition under Plato, and later Aristotle, introduced a division into traditional perceptions of the nature of man, his environment,

1. 1986, Picador, London
2. Picador, London
3. The author lived and worked with the Bariba for two years.

and the spiritual. A hierarchical perception of life was developed, with God, or the Gods, at the top, spirits next, then human beings, then animals, and finally remaining matter. In this schema, nature was stripped of its spirit presence, and spiritual and intellectual realities had priority over matter, which often was not valued very highly. Humans were placed at the top of the hierarchy of nature. Thus the spiritual was seen as something distant and removed from humans' immediate environs. Nature's value was reduced to a functional resource base, existing to serve the needs of humankind, nature's superior.

*1.3 Science Reinforces Western Dualistic Perceptions*
This view has unfortunately been shared by many of the influential shapers of Western culture, a culture whose understanding of life and spirituality has come to be dominated by a scientific, mechanistic view of the world. Blinkered by remarkable scientific and technological developments, modern culture has lost sight of the essence of humanity and nature – that of the integrity of the spirit, nature and humanity. Thus the first radically anthropocentric society has been borne.

From Aristotle on, men have felt compelled to arrange nature neatly in hierarchy, unlocking its underlying mysteries and mechanics, and exploiting it for their own benefit. We see evidence of this hierarchical division also in humankind where it has given rise to gender, class, caste and racial distinctions and discriminations. Linnaeus, the eighteenth-century biologist, in his publication *Species Plantarum*, was the first to catalogue all of nature into the system of species still in use today. Neatly classified and labeled, man then sought to unlock nature's secrets and exploit them. However, the intrinsic spiritual dimension of the earth cannot be dissected and inserted into empirical sets of equations and formulae. Modern science can only go so far.

The scientific community itself acknowledges that it has captured but a fragment of the bigger picture. The wave-particle dual nature of light is probably the best known example of conflicting scientific theory. In the nineteenth century, experiments by Maxwell, Hertz, and others, proved that light travels in energy waves. Yet, Einstein's quantum theory in the 1920s proved it travels in discrete energy particles. Which is true? This depends which experiment you carry out. The current scientific consensus is that in some circumstances light is wave in nature, and in others particulate. The picture is obviously far from complete. Some scientists have the foresight to allow for the unknown, the 'uncertain'. Werner Heisenberg's 'Uncertainty Principle' is one of the cornerstones of modern quantum physics. It states, roughly speaking, that all physical quantities that can be observed are subject to unpredictable fluctuations, so that their values are not precisely defined. This uncertainty is inherent in nature, due to a limitation in what is known about these systems, and not the result of technological limitations in measurement. Heisenberg himself[4] cautions that 'we have to remember that what we observe is not nature in itself but nature exposed to our method of questioning' (p 46), and again 'But even if complete clarity has been achieved in this way (using a mathematical equation), it is not known how accurately the set of concepts describes reality' (p 96).

So, even with the achievements of the keenest minds in the world, our understanding of nature is seriously deficient, in many cases flawed. Yet this understanding is what drives the modern, industrial, technological world we live in. From the alarm bell that wakes us in the morning to the hot cocoa that lulls us to sleep, we rely on the products of technological advancement to take us through the day. The danger is that, in irresponsibly exploiting what is in effect only a tiny functional fragment of the big-

4. *Physics and Philosophy*, 1990, Penguin, London

ger picture, we risk not only denying ourselves the benefits of the bigger picture, but also, more importantly, destroying it for others. Moreover, the reductionist, mechanistic analysis that underlies conventional scientific method also underlies, and has shaped and moulded our current economic and political systems, leaving little room for the deeper, less measurable elements to find expression. Ignoring these elements has proved fatal. The current ecological, economic, and political crisis is the result.

Science will never lead us to the ultimate truth about nature. But this is not to say it has no place. In illuminating the complexities of the universe science plays a valuable role. However we should remain aware of its and our own limits in this regard.

## 1.4 Judaeo-Christian Teaching – Ethno- or Eco-Centred

Western dualistic perceptions have also left a significant imprint on Judaeo-Christian tradition. Within this tradition, the biblical story tells of creation and deliverance, and the chief actor is God, 'who created the heavens and stretched them out, who spread forth the earth and what comes from it, and who gave breath to the people upon it and spirit to those who walk in it' (Is 42:5). God's concern for the whole of creation is revealed throughout the scriptures. The land was to be kept undefiled and unpolluted (Num 35:33-34) and was to be allowed to rest periodically (Lev 25:11).

God's blessing to man and woman following their creation in Genesis, 'Be fruitful, multiply, fill the earth and conquer it. Be masters of the fish of the sea, the birds of heaven and all living animals of the earth' (Gen 1:26-28), has, however, led to much debate and controversy within the church. Selective interpretations of the command to be 'masters' of the earth and to 'conquer' it have had a profound impact on the way Jews and Christians have related to the natural world. Indeed the church has sustained much criticism over what is seen by some as its arrogance towards nature and its muted voice in the face of the current environmental crisis.

Fr Seán McDonagh however, in his book, *The Greening of the Church*,[5] argues that this command cannot be interpreted as a licence for humans to take control of and transform the natural world according to their needs (Chapter 4). He argues that it calls for humans to be 'stewards' of creation and claims that 'Even though in the biblical view men and women are somewhat segregated from the non-human components of the earth, there is recognition that they are totally dependent on the natural world, and that this is an interrelated and interdependent world with its own laws which reflects the will of the Creator' (p 119).

The founder of the Jesuit order, St Ignatius of Loyola, also stressed the interdependence of humans and the universe. He wrote that a person cannot find God unless he finds him through his environment and, conversely, that his relationship to the environment will be out of balance unless he also relates to God.[6]

Some centuries later Teilhard de Chardin, SJ, theologian and scientist, bridging the duality between science and theology, presented an intellectual framework for a more creative dialogue between the two. Followers of this framework, like Thomas Berry, have used these insights to develop a more eco-centred approach. Observing the geological and biological change caused by technology, Berry calls for a mutually enhancing relationship between humans and nature. Berry speaks of moving from the techno sphere into an ecozoic era. The challenge now becomes how to live responsibly and sustainably in this ecozoic era. This presents technological, political and economic challenges.

5. 1990, Claretian Publications, Philippine Edition
6. Cited in 'Our Responsibility for God's Creation' (p.6), Address by Fr Peter-Hans Kolvenbach, SJ, Superior General of the Society of Jesus, at the opening of Arrupe College Jesuit School of Philosophy and Humanities in Harare, Zimbabwe, August 1998.

## 2. The Environmental Crisis Escalates

Harmony with the earth is hardly evident in the environmental crisis we currently face, however. And as the crisis worsens, in the face of political and individual inaction, it is the earth and the poor who suffer the most.

As we sit in traffic jams here in Ireland, radio reports bring us news of yet more local opposition to proposed waste disposal facilities whilst the volumes we produce increases exponentially. In the year 2000 alone we produced almost 2.3 million tonnes of household and commercial waste, an increase of over sixty percent in five years. It is now estimated that almost six hundred kilograms of waste are produced by each person in this state each year.[7] Yet only 12.2% of this is recycled, a proportion considerably distant from the government's target of 35%. Water, air and habitat quality are also declining. Some trends are as follows:

---

**The Irish Environment: The Statistics**

*Biodiversity and Nature*
18 species of birds are in rapid decline whilst a further 76 species are under threat, indicating severe pressure on their habitats.

*Water Quality*
Over 30% of river channels are polluted.
Ground water in counties Carlow, Cork, Kerry, Louth and Waterford are polluted.

*Air Quality*
Under international obligations we are committed to limiting greenhouse gases to 13% above 1990 levels. However by 2000 our emissions had already increased 24% above these levels.

*Transport*
The total number of vehicles increased by 60% between 1990 and 2000 with private cars accounting for the major part of this increase. 60% of people travelling to work do so by car.

*Source : 'Environment in Focus 2002', EPA 2002*

---

7. *Environment in Focus 2002, Key Environmental Indicators for Ireland*, EPA, 2002.

Elsewhere too, human activities are damaging and destroying what remains of the natural world around us. Water tables are falling on every continent, half of the world's original forest area has been destroyed over the last century, atmospheric concentrations of carbon dioxide have climbed to the highest level in 150,000 years, and the diversity of life forms is increasingly threatened. All of this linked to our excessive demands: From 1950 to 1997, the use of lumber tripled, that of paper increased sixfold, the fish catch increased nearly fivefold, grain consumption nearly tripled, fossil fuel burning nearly quadrupled, and air and water pollutants multiplied severalfold.[8] The unfortunate reality is that the economy continues to expand, but the ecosystem on which it depends does not, creating increasingly stressed relationships.

## 2.1 The Poor Suffer the Most

As the seas lose their wealth, the soil its fertility, as the rivers become polluted, and life's diversity is destroyed, it is the poor who suffer the most. These are the people most affected by desertification, by floods, storms and harvest failures caused by global warming. The overwhelming majority of those who die each year from air and water pollution are poor people. They generally live nearest to dirty factories, busy roads, and waste dumps. The irony is that even though the poor bear the brunt of environmental damage, they are seldom the principal orchestrators of this damage. It is the rich who contribute the most to global warming, the rich who pollute more, the rich who generate the most waste, and the rich who put the greatest stress on nature's sink. And in a cruel twist, as a result of increasing impoverishment and the absence of alternatives, a growing number of poor people are being forced to place unprecedented pressure on the natural resource base as they struggle to survive. It is a downward spiral; people in

8. *State of the World*, 1998, Worldwatch Institute, New York

poverty are forced to deplete resources to survive, yet this degradation further impoverishes them.

These are limited resources which must be equitably, responsibly and respectfully shared by all. This is not happening. In the industrialised world, in Ireland, our current consumption levels are exorbitant and damaging.[9] Globally, consumption of goods and services will top US$24 trillion this year, six times the figure for 1975, yet over one billion people fail to meet even their basic consumption requirements. The average African household today consumes less than it did 25 years ago. The 20% of the world's people in the highest income countries account for 86% of total private consumption, the poorest 1.3%. The richest fifth consume: 45% of all meat and fish, the poorest 5%; 58% of total energy, the poorest less than 4%; and 84% of all paper, the poorest 1.1%.[10] Clearly there is a need for a different pattern of consumption, a pattern which reflects our respect for the earth and all its peoples rather than a select privileged and powerful few.

## 2.2 Current Policies Exacerbate the Crisis

Current efforts at addressing this crisis are not succeeding because they continue to fall within the parameters of the modem scientifically moulded patterns of production, distribution, consumption, trade and development which, blind to the integrity of creation and humanity, are destroying the regenerative capacity of the biosphere on which they feed.

### 2.2.1 International Commitments

The Earth Summit in Rio in 1992, followed by the Kyoto Protocol, as it was originally conceived in 1997, was never going to solve climate change but it was a start. Its most

9. see *Environment in Focus 2002, Key Environmental Indicators for Ireland,* EPA, 2002
10. *Human Development Report,* 1998, UNDP, OUP, New York

important factor was the requirement to industrialised countries to accept legally binding targets to reduce green-house gas emissions.[11] Whilst the total reduction required was far less than that advocated by climatologists it was nonetheless a move in the right direction. However, with the withdrawal of United States in 2001 this modest target has been severely weakened. The Bush administration jus-tified its withdrawal on the grounds that the Protocol was unfair in that it exempts developing nations. Yet the US, with just 5% of the world's population, produces a quarter of the world's carbon emissions, more than any other country: eleven times more per head of population than China; twenty times more than India; and three hundred times more than Mozambique.[12] At these levels US partici-pation in targeting emission reductions is imperative.

---

**Points about Global Energy Use and Climate Change**

• Since 1950, global coal use has more than doubled, global oil use has risen eight-fold, and the use of natural gas has grown 12 times.

• Ten times more energy is spent on growing crops using industrial-ised high-input systems compared with a sustainable farming system.

• Climate change will cause an additional 170 million people to be living in severely water-stressed areas by the year 2050.

• Europe's off-shore wind potential in waters of thirty metres depth or less could supply all of the continent's power.

---

## 2.2.2 Economic Policy

Whilst most of the world's governments have now accept-ed the reality of environmental pollution and degradation, hardly any have made the link to the macro-economic

---

11. The IPCC (Intergovernmental Panel on Climate Change), a body of scientists, economists and policy makers which the UN brought together to examine likely causes and consequences of climate change has, after some 12 years collection and analysis of data, concluded that most of the observed warming over the last 50 years is likely to have been due to the increase in greenhouse gas concentrations which is 'attributable to human activities', (IPCC 3rd Assessment Report, March 2001).
12. *The Ecologist Report – Climate Change*, November 2001

policies pursued in their countries. An unfettered drive for economic growth and ever-increasing production and consumption has severely damaged and depleted many of the earth's life-systems. Clearly a finite natural resource base cannot feed infinite growth in production and consumption. Yet these are our expectations. We all want, and feel we deserve, more.

However, in a world of limited natural resources, our respect for this life means that growth cannot be pursued indefinitely. All boats cannot rise together. In fact, one person's wealth is the consequence of another's exploitation and poverty, together with the depletion of a variety of life systems. To achieve a balance the objective becomes, not wealth creation, but wealth distribution.

Globalisation, a term we hear much debate about these days, involving the dismantling of barriers to trade and investment, has led to vast increases in demand for energy – for both production and transport. Global shipping has grown approximately ten-fold by weight since 1950, consuming 140 million tonnes of fuel each year worldwide, more than the annual consumption of the entire Middle East. World air cargo grew by 280% between 1985 and 1997 and overland freight transport has also increased dramatically with Europe, for example, experiencing a tripling of trans-border truck traffic from 1970 to 1997. Trade transportation is now responsible for the consumption of over an eighth of world oil production.[13]

### 2.2.3 Access to Food
Each year, 80 million more people require food. Yet how is this being addressed? International policy is promoting the consolidation of the world's biological resources in the hands of a small number of transnational corporations (TNCs). Beginning by taking over smaller seed producing

---

13. *The Ecologist Report – Climate Change*, November 2001

companies, TNCs have now successfully lobbied many governments to pass biopatenting legislation which allows them to purchase monopoly rights to both seeds and agricultural practices. The European Parliament adopted a biopatenting Directive in 1998 to which all member states are bound, and pressure is on poorer countries to develop similar legislation under the TRIPS provision of the WTO.[14]

The argument is that these corporations can produce food more efficiently. Yet food insecurity is not a problem of production. There is enough food to feed the world. The problem is distribution and access to resources. In any case it is questionable whether a company which genetically engineers seeds to be sterile following harvest, thereby forcing farmers to repurchase each year, is really interested in increased crop yields or increased profit margins.[15] This monopolisation is indeed a very worrying development for both consumers and the environment, and certainly one which is antithetical to an eco-centred approach to development.

In addition, the loss of biodiversity – estimated at 10,000 species annually – destroys potential sources of food for the growing population. Despite the varied diets around the world, humans currently only use 1% of the known species of nourishment. Agricultural policies favouring intensive monocultural production over more traditional mixed systems are exacerbating this biodestruction, and with it many more potential sources of nourishment.

14. The WTO, formerly known as GATT, has governed the international trade system since the end of World War II. Its purpose is to dismantle trade barriers. The new Trade Related Intellectual Property provision (TRIPS) obligates all WTO signatories to adopt minimum intellectual property standards (patents and copyrights) for all plants and micro-organisms.

15. In March 1998, the US Department of Agriculture and the Delta Pine and Land Co obtained a patent on a technological process which permits the creation of sterile seed by genetically engineering a plant's DNA to kill its own embryos. The patent applies to plants and seeds of all species and ensures that farmers cannot save or re-use their seed. The technology is known as the 'Terminator Gene'.

## 3. A CHANGE IN VALUES

Clearly some radical changes are required at policy level
to reduce the ravages of unfettered exploitation of all life.
However, many of the changes required are more fundamental than mere policy changes. They require a shift
away from the secular, mechanistic, utilitarian view of
nature to an appreciation of its complexity and its connection
to us. In short, they require a fundamental shift in values.
However you cannot legislate values. Values emerge from
the cultural ground of experience. And this experience is
coloured, shaped and interpreted through the lens of conviction and respect.

These values can then form the basis for both political
and economic policies, and for fundamental changes in
the way we live our own everyday lives.

### 3.1 Individual Responsibility

Because over-consumption and excess waste is depleting
resources and accentuating injustice we, as individuals,
have a responsibility to redesign our lifestyles. An eco-
centred faith is one that does justice through individual actions. There is no clearer message of how we perceive our
relationship with the earth than how we choose to live our
lives. If we are to be honest to our beliefs we must do all
we can to ensure equity in the use of, and the distribution
of resources. We have a responsibility to reduce our consumption and to avoid the use of toxic substances. A number of ways we can do this is suggested below, but all that
is really required is a little bit of thoughtfulness and prag-
matism in our daily activities.

### • Energy

Energy conservation is an important way to reduce our
use of fossil fuels. This will help conserve limited resources
and reduce 'greenhouse gases' (carbon dioxide, chloro-
fluorocarbons (CFCs), and nitrous oxide). More effective

insulation in buildings, warmer clothing, electricity from renewable sources (solar, hydro, wind, biomass), low watt light bulbs, and high efficiency electrical appliances are all ways of conserving energy.

• *Transport*
A very contentious issue in these Celtic Tiger-carbon-monoxide ridden times, particularly among city-dwellers. For short journeys it is healthier and more enjoyable to walk or cycle. Cycle lanes are becoming more common and, in the city, it is often faster to reach many destinations by bike. Public transport is also an increasingly viable option, both in cities and for national travel.

• *Water*
In our climate there seems to be a lot of it around yet with increasing levels of pollution, clean water is a scarce resource. Reduce water use in the home – don't leave taps running, water plants with dish or bathwater. Every time we flush the toilet we flush away 12 litres of drinking water. Placing bricks in the cistern can reduce the volume flushed away each time.

• *Conserve and Recycle*
We should aim to reduce our waste as much as possible. Promote recycling (glass, aluminium, paper) initiatives in your area. Avoid disposable goods (styrofoam cups, plastic cutlery, paper towels...) and buy reliable goods that will last and can be repaired.

• *Exercise Consumer Pressure*
Avoid buying products like plastics which are non-biodegradeable, or goods wrapped in wasteful packaging. Check the sources of your products (wood and paper from sustainable forests, fairly traded products, locally grown organic foodstuffs, clothing and manufactured goods –

many cheaper goods come from factories exploiting women and children for long hours with very low wages). Shop in locally owned and run shops and, where possible, buy locally produced goods.

• *Avoid Toxic Substances*
Avoid or minimise use of insect sprays, pesticides, detergents, toilet disinfectants and toilet paper containing toxic substances. Oil, paint products or other toxic substances should not be flushed down the sink. Buy phosphate-free biodegradeable soaps and detergents. Unprocessed food free of chemical additives is generally more nutritious and healthy.

• *Responsibilise local industry*
Together with members of your community ensure local companies in your area minimise the use of toxic chemicals and do not dispose of them illegally.

• *Ethical Investments*
Invest surplus money in 'ethical' investments, ie. avoid investing in companies that pursue objectionable and harmful practices – armaments, nuclear power, environmental pollution, violation of labour rights, speculative investors …). Support companies which can prove they act in a caring manner towards society and the environment.

It is imperative that our change in values, reflecting a shift of focus from the individual to the collective, from our personal needs to those of our environs, find voice in our everyday choices, decisions, and actions. Respect, for the earth, its spirit, and its peoples, will only then become real. A life lived without this respect is a life not worth living at all.

## 4. Conclusion

Western dualism has fuelled a system of development which has led to the current ecological and humanitarian crisis. Efforts at a global political and economic level have fallen far short of resolving the problem because they have not been accompanied by a critical shift in values. We have failed to protect the life systems of this planet and we have failed to protect ourselves. If the beauty of the land is disfigured, if the fertility of the soil is lost, if the rivers are polluted, if living species disappear, then the integral life of humans is endangered and the human soul shrivels. The spiritual void that remains feeds an unjust, inequitable system which fails us all.

If, however, we pull ourselves back from the edge, back from the divide we have created between ourselves and the earth, we can rediscover the value of both the earth and ourselves. Respectfully taking our place in this integral society, we can once again learn to look outwards. A faith that does justice is a faith that diverts us away from this pathway to self-destruction. It is a faith that challenges us to rethink our role and impact on this earth. It is a faith that calls for fundamental changes in the way we live our lives so that the wealth of the earth may be sustainably and equitably available to all. Only when we once again begin to look outwards, to respectfully take our place in a wider, integral society, will we genuinely begin to effectively address the growing environmental, economic and political crisis, and deliver evidence of a committed faith in action.

# CHAPTER THIRTEEN

# Two Challenges for Social Spirituality

*Séamus Murphy SJ*

## Spirituality

Spirituality is 'in' today. It is popular and 'politically correct' in a way that religion is not. There are all sorts of spirituality available, from those of the major religions, through the quasi-religious diversity of New Age options, to the explicitly non-religious types of spirituality. Some take it with great seriousness and build their lives on it, some use it as a comfort and support when needed, and some add it on as a kind of fashion accessory.

There are many reasons for its current popularity. In the information age, greater awareness and access to the spiritual heritage of other cultures has generated interest in them. There is a hunger for meaning and transcendence, particularly in the wealthier parts of the world, where the established religions appear no longer to give a compelling meaning. For some, spirituality is the human face of religion; for others, it is the attractive post-modern alternative to religion. The DIY nature of spirituality permits an *à la carte* approach: whatever your taste, whether your mix is the Enneagram, the I Ching and belief in angels, or you like to combine Zen techniques with Carmelite spirituality, all things appear possible.

## Social concern

Traditionally, the focus of social concern has been with making the world a better place and meeting people's basic needs for shelter, work, education, health-care and a share in the world's wealth, particularly those of the poor and excluded. From this perspective, spirituality is relevant to the degree to which it promotes that goal. While spirituality will not directly solve such problems as world hunger or homelessness, it should make people more concerned and passionate about such issues so that they act to address them. In other words, spirituality's contribution to social justice is to make persons more just.

However, social activists tend to have a very restrictive notion of the just person, since they take a just person to be simply one engaged with issues of social justice.[1] But there's a great deal more to it than that, and unless there is some openness to that fact, no effective connection between the social and the spiritual can be made. Spirituality's primary focus must be on the person, on her search for meaning, transcendence and God, on the depth dimension of a human life. In no way should this search exclude the social dimension. Here, the spiritual life and the moral life come together and cannot be separated. The nexus of the link between the social and the spiritual is the person.

Two aspects of the contemporary spiritual scene are alarming, constituting serious challenges to any Christian (or Jewish or Muslim) spirituality committed to social justice. First, much spirituality is excessively psychological in orientation, inward-oriented at times even to being narcissistic, and neglectful of the social and the civic dimensions of personal being. Second, some New Age ideas of nature, currently spreading among Christians, radically undermine Christian notions of justice.

*First challenge: inward, therapeutic spirituality*
The quest for a spirituality arises from people's need for a 'depth' dimension to their lives. It is intimately connected

1. The presuppositions about justice underlying social critique of recent decades are utilitarian. This leads to holding that justice is first and last about good social outcomes, about producing a just society. Actions and persons are to be evaluated solely as means to that end.

with the question that is at the heart of recent developments in ethical theory: what is the good life for a person? what is admirable, worthwhile, truly of value in a human life?

Some contemporary spirituality is trivial, being little more than a fashion accessory. The mark of the trivial spirituality is that it does not propose any serious change or reformed way of life for the person. Serious spirituality does propose ideals to live by and models to imitate. Thus, spirituality touches closely on what it is to be a particular kind of person.

Like the other great religions, Christianity combines spirituality with social commitment. In all the great religions, the spiritual life and the moral life go together. In the case of Christianity, their common element is the imitation of Christ, personal transformation so that one becomes a new creation, thinking, feeling and acting as Jesus Christ would, moved by his Spirit. Herein lies the Christian model of the just person.

It is not possible to have the virtue of justice, without to some extent having other virtues as well. One cannot be a just person, without also being a person of practical intelligence and judgement (prudence in older terminology), of moderation and balance (temperance), and of courage (fortitude). These are the hinge virtues, the key-qualities without which a person is not likely to be effective in helping to make society more just. Other qualities or virtues include kindness, openness to and respect for other persons, and sexual integrity (chastity), to mention but a few.

Of particular importance in the Christian view of the good person are the virtues of faith, hope and charity, which are gifts of grace. With respect to social justice, the virtue of faith is a belief in God's plan of salvation, a plan which embraces the establishment of a world of justice and peace, even though one may not live to see it oneself. Hope is a strong and persevering desire for that kingdom, and a resistance to the sense of futility of ever righting social wrongs. Charity is love of God, the supreme good, for his own sake, and love for others that goes beyond the natural love for family and friends and fellow-tribesmen.

While some of this may sound old-fashioned, I suggest that it is anything but irrelevant or redundant. As noted above, in recent years the most popular spirituality has been too inward in orientation and excessively reliant on a therapeutic model of spirituality. Nor have the Christian churches escaped the trend by any means. This has generated the widespread impression that the main goal of spirituality is, first, to make one feel good about oneself, and second, to reassure one that one's psychological history is enormously important, being the repository of one's identity as a person and of one's most authentic values. These significant cultural developments have been well delineated in Philip Rieff's classic work, *The Triumph of the Therapeutic* (New York 1966) and in Christopher Lasch's *The Culture of Narcissism* (New York 1979).

As might be imagined, the trend is most noticeable in middle and upper income groups. Robert Putnam's studies on the decline of bowling clubs and other civic groups, along with Christopher Lasch's, *The Revolt of the Elites and the Betrayal of Democracy* (New York 1995) are representative of a rising concern among informed observers about the reduction of social involvement by the middle and upper classes. The dominant trends in contemporary spirituality do nothing to discourage (and, by default, even mildly encourage) such withdrawal and detachment. Of course we must all acknowledge our 'brokenness' as persons, but the emphasis on building awareness of 'brokenness' and fragility can have the effect of moving people away from the outward-oriented challenge of the gospel. The idea that the spiritual is much closer to the psychological than to the social has become deep-rooted and widespread today.

It is precisely here that the virtue ethics tradition can play a bridging role.[2] Its focus is on the person, not on society as such; but it does not have the strongly inward, psychological bias of much contemporary spirituality. The virtues are as much outward-oriented as inward-oriented, and are a valuable corrective in this area. Temperance, courage, practical intelligence, justice, compassion, fairness, civic commitment and social concern are the kind of admirable personal qualities or virtues which good spirituality should foster.

*Second challenge: the ideology of nature-worship*
The second challenge is rather more serious, and as yet very few Christian writers have faced up to it. Neglecting to do so, however, will probably have significant implications for social justice.

One's spirituality is connected to one's overall worldview and to one's scientific, religious, and common-sense beliefs. Anti-intellectualism about religion has infected many Christians over the last thirty years, typically expressed along the lines of 'Well, it doesn't really matter what beliefs people have, as long as they love one another and do good.' This is wrong, for two reasons. First, people act on their beliefs: believing that Jews are sub-human, that unborn human beings have no rights, that the state has no right to take money off me in taxes, that my God will not accept me unless I look out for the poor, are all likely to make a difference to my behaviour. Second, one can't love others and do good unless one has some ideas or beliefs about who, what, and how to love. Some notions of loving include forgiveness of enemies, and some do not. Christian love is not the same as instinctive natural love, as Jesus noted in the Sermon on the Mount.

---

2. See Jean Porter, 'Virtue ethics and its significance for spirituality', *The Way* supplement 88 (1997); Séamus Murphy, 'The many ways of justice', *Studies in the Spirituality of Jesuits* (1994).

Many western Christians do not understand their own faith and, having been taught by a relativist media that 'beliefs don't matter', they often have little incentive to deepen their understanding, so they see no great problem in mixing Christian and non-Christian spiritualities. This is not necessarily a bad thing; in some cases, it enriches, deepens and complements Christian faith. Sometimes, however, what is mixed in is radically incompatible with the Christian message or any of the Abrahamic faiths. This can have significant consequences for social justice.

The notion of social justice in the Abrahamic faiths of Judaism, Christianity and Islam is grounded in the following ideas:

1. God created the world freely out of love,
2. making the human person in his own image and likeness,
3. who, in consequence, has transcendent dignity and inestimable value.
4. God calls us to relationship with him, and the purpose and fulfilment of the human person is to be found in relationship with God, expressed in praising, reverencing and serving him,
5. an intrinsic part of which is loving one's neighbours as oneself, treating them with justice, compassion and mercy, and seeking to build a society of justice and peace (in the Christian framework, this is further specified as imitating Christ).
6. The nature of the human person is such that her happiness can be achieved only through an integrated pursuit of that purpose.
7. The purpose of the rest of creation is to enable the human person to achieve those goals.
8. God's providence will ensure the ultimate victory of good over evil at the culmination of history, and in the cosmic struggle between good and evil taking place in history, the human person cannot but make a decisive

choice in that struggle, expressed by her choosing (or refusing to choose) whether or not to live out the implications of God's call.

Much of what is found in contemporary New Age, particularly in the nature-oriented spirituality, rejects some or all of those claims. The claims listed manifest a certain order to our loving and our doing justice, and that order is different from the one proposed by the nature-religions.

As the great literature of the world indicates, love is mysterious, and one's understanding of what love is, of what and how one is to love, can make a great difference. In the Abrahamic faiths, God is to be loved totally and above all else, including oneself, as the only object capable and worthy of receiving such love. The neighbour is to be loved as much as but no more than oneself, and everything else is to be treated respectfully and used as means to the two loves mentioned. The types of spirituality found in the Abrahamic faiths are essentially about helping to shape one into the kind of person who understands that vision and lives it out in obedience to the God who has revealed himself.

*Mother Nature, Goddess Gaea*
The most striking thing about much contemporary spirituality is its orientation to nature. As a result of various factors, notably the ecological movement, we have become aware of the interlocking nature of earth's ecosystem, its fragility, the non-replaceability of many of its resources, and the long-term alterations which have occurred to it as a result of industrialisation and consumption of fossil fuels. There is a moral imperative to avoid wastefulness, to recycle, and to preserve the environment as much as possible. A well-rounded spirituality would encourage people to live simply, avoid acquisitiveness and conspicuous consumption, and value life in all its forms. 'Live simply so

that others might live' is a slogan whose relevance is, if anything, increasing. The social dimension of fasting in the Abrahamic faiths (e.g. Lent, Ramadan) is obvious.

There is a down-side to the focus on nature, and here it is not just in New Age, but has spread into Christian circles. New Age includes such explicitly nature-religions as Wicca, Neo-paganism, and witchcraft (the white variety) in various forms. At least they are quite clear about their being nature-religions, and about nature as such being the object of worship or reverence. However, certain elements of Christian spirituality are shading into this, but without realising the implications of doing so.[3] This has appeared in the form of ecology-as-religion, involving such ideas as:

- God is not personal, but is instead a kind of energy or life-force of the universe. The significance of this point is that God is not to be thought of as having conscious intelligence or free will, in any sense analogous to that of human persons.
- God (or Nature) loves everything; everything is 'good', and is to be affirmed as such. Notions of evil, guilt, sin, etc., are oppressive and irrelevant.
- Every part of the universe, whether animal, vegetable, or mineral is just as valuable, morally and spiritually, as the human person. To hold the traditional monotheist view that human beings are special is 'species-ism', and to follow Genesis 1:28 and hold that human beings have been given dominion over the earth is patriarchal and oppressive.
- The birds and the bees, the flowers and the trees, are the real poor today, and have just as much a moral claim on us (even to the point of having 'rights') as do the homeless or the destitute.

There is a spirituality here; and it is incompatible with the Abrahamic faiths. It is pantheistic, in that it identifies

3. This applies to some of the recent literature on Celtic spirituality.

God with nature, or with the life-principle or dynamism in nature: on this view, minerals, plants, animals and humans are all part of God. The problem with being part of God, however, is that one can't have a relationship with such a God.

Another problem with identifying God with nature is that morality and justice become meaningless. This is overlooked because of the romantic view of nature involved in contemporary nature-worship, involving looking at nature through rose-tinted spectacles. Yet this is selective: it fits with Wordsworth's benevolent Mother Nature, but not with Thomas Hardy's grim forces of nature, or Tennyson's line about 'Nature, red in tooth and claw'. Nature is not just beautiful flowers, but also Venus fly-traps; not just beautiful sunsets, but also the asteroid hurtling towards us with our name written on it. Nature is as much the carnivore as the herbivore. As Nietzsche rightly remarked once: 'Let us beware of attributing to [the universe] heartlessness and unreason or their opposites: it is neither perfect nor beautiful, nor noble … None of our aesthetic and moral judgments apply to it' (*The gay science*, III,109).

## The implications for social justice

The differences between nature-religion and the Abrahamic faiths include the following.

1. Nature-religions devalue human persons, relative to other living things. It is not unknown for some people, ostensibly Christian, to hold that, as a general rule and not just by way of exception, unused land should be turned into nature preserves, rather than made available for something like social housing. The implication for social justice is obvious. It arises from a rejection of a key-notion in the Abrahamic faiths: that the human being, unlike other living things on this planet, was made in the image and likeness of God, and given

dominion over the earth. The dominion is not absolute, being a form of stewardship: humans do not have the right to destroy and waste wantonly. But in the Abrahamic faiths, planet Earth and what it contains exist for the benefit of human beings.

2. The notion that the human person is special and has inestimable value is a distinctively religious notion, and liable to lapse in a sufficiently secularised society. This is reflected in the fact that some contemporary bioethicists hold that a new-born baby has less right to life than an adult orangutan, since it has less of a sense of its own interests than the orangutan. Furthermore, ecology-as-religion, holding that it is the species, rather than the individual member of the species that has value, tends to apply that to human beings. This leads to a logic of eugenics giving primacy to the improvement of the species, even involving weeding out the weaker specimens and genetically impaired. The implications of all this for social justice should positively leap out at Christians.[4]

3. The value of the species is not rejected by the Abrahamic faiths: but it is very secondary to the key-notion of the unique value of the person. Indeed, compared to the value of the person, the human species as such has very slight value. The human person has value because he or she is like God, and because he or she has intelligence and will and is capable of relating to God in an inter-personal way. The command of the Bible, both Old and New Testament, is that 'you shall love the Lord your God with all your heart and strength, and your neighbour as yourself'. Why love your neighbour? Because he or she is a fairly valuable member of

4. The writings of Peter Singer, professor of bioethics at Princeton, are particularly significant here. He is rightly emphatic that the notion of the sanctity of human life is rooted in the Judeo-Christian religious ethic.

the species? Surely not. Again, the implications for social justice of the monotheist faith is that the neighbour, because he or she is a person, is an image or ikon of God and so of infinite worth.

4. There is a negative side to attributing rights to animals. Of course, animals ought not be treated cruelly, abused or wantonly killed. But rights are normally correlative with duties. It makes little sense, from the point of view of ethical theory, to assign rights (potentially equal to those of humans) to a species which is incapable of being assigned duties. To claim that I have violated a deer's rights by shooting it would imply that the bear who kills it for meat has also violated its rights; this is incoherent. More seriously, to divorce rights from correlative duties is a formula for social disintegration, which certainly involves social injustice.

5. In the worldview of the Abrahamic faiths, there are objective moral facts, ultimately grounded in the God who has revealed himself as goodness, justice and love, and who has given us a moral nature in our ability to choose. Thus, the wrongness of rape derives from the inherent nature of the act, not from people's subjective feeling about it or society's saying it is wrong (both of which may vary with the culture). Nature-worship can only affirm the goodness of nature. Since that same Nature is also 'red in tooth and claw', with carnivores devouring herbivores, it implies accepting whatever happens 'naturally'. In other words, moral values have no ultimate grounding there. Even when it affirms the goodness of nature, it is not moral goodness. If anything, nature-worship is ultimately more likely to support the rule of the strong over the weak, reflecting the kind of spirituality one might derive from the novels of Ayn Rand (*The Fountain-head, Atlas Shrugged,* etc) or the writings of Nietzsche, who perceptively saw that democracy and socialism were rooted in Christianity.

Both challenges are serious, the more so because few seem to realise the implications of recent developments. Precisely because spirituality is so 'in' today, the direction it takes will have significant implications for the kind of society that will emerge in the future.

# The Contributors

JIM CORKERY is an Irish Jesuit form Limerick now working in Dublin. He teaches Theology at the Milltown Institute.

BERNADETTE FLANAGAN is a Presentation sister and head of the Department of Spirituality at the Milltown Institute of Theology and Philosophy. She has published *The Spirit of the City* (Veritas, 1999).

NIAMH GAYNOR is a freelance writer, researcher and facilitator.

PATRICIA HIGGINS currently works as the coordinator of Slí Eile North Inner City Volunteers. She is a former fulltime volunteer with JVC (Jesuit Volunteer Communities) and has been involved in the training and support of full-time, part-time and overseas volunteers.

BRIAN LENNON is a Jesuit priest who works in Northern Ireland with Community Dialogue.

PETER MCVERRY is a Jesuit priest. He is Director of the Arrupe Society, an organisation working for homeless young people in Dublin.

CATHY MOLLOY is a theology lecturer presently working as a researcher at the Jesuit Centre for Faith and Justice.

LAURENCE MURPHY has been involved in Jesuit formation work both in Ireland and in Rome. After six years as Provincial he is at present Director of the Jesuit Centre of Spirituality at Manresa, Dublin.

SEAMUS MURPHY is a philosophy lecturer at the Milltown Institute and writes frequently on public policy issues. He is a Jesuit.

SEAMUS O'GORMAN is an Irish Jesuit. He has spent some time working in Zambia and has most recently been working at the Jesuit Centre for Faith and Justice as part of the International Jesuit Network for Development, (IJND). He is currently doing doctoral studies in Leuven in relation to Christian theology and international debt.

EUGENE QUINN is an actuary and currently is Director of the Jesuit Centre for Faith and Justice in Dublin. He worked in Bosnia with the Jesuit Refugee Services between 1998 and 2000.

BILL TONER is a former Director of the Jesuit Centre for Faith and Justice. He currently works in Province central administration in the Jesuit Order in Dublin.

AILEEN WALSH is a psychologist and spiritual director. She lectures in Pastoral Theology at the Milltown Institute.